My Hutterite *Life*

by **Lisa Marie Stahl**

foreword and photography by Michael Crummett

D0112134

FARCOUNTRY
PRESS

Dedication

To my faithful readers who, because of
their curiosity, have helped me open a
door that I thought was impossible.

The publisher gratefully acknowledges the assistance of
Karen Ogden, Lisa's editor, and the *Great Falls Tribune*.

Text © 2003 by Lisa Marie Stahl
Photographs © 2003 by Michael Crummett and Karen Ogden
© 2003 by Farcountry Press

All articles by Lisa Marie Stahl originally appeared in the
Great Falls Tribune, Great Falls, Montana, 2000-2003.

ISBN 10: 1-56037-264-8
ISBN 13: 978-1-56037-264-6

For more information on Farcountry Press books, write Farcountry Press, P.O. Box 5630,
Helena, MT 59604 or call (800) 821-3874 or visit www.farcountrypress.com

Created, produced, and designed in the United States of America.
Printed in the United States of America.
10 09 08 07 06   3 4 5 6 7

Table of Contents

⁙

Heaven on Earth

❦

Foreword by Michael Crummett

On our walks of life and circles of travel, we often encounter those dear, distinctive souls of faith who, through their sameness, dare to be different.

At local hardware shops and implement dealerships, we see the bearded men who are uniformly outfitted in black from head to toe.

At the nearby Kmart or Wal-Mart stores, we meet head-on a vanload of women draped in the predictable patterns of black, dark blues, olives, and maroons.

At farmers' markets that sprout up across Montana's summer landscape, we anxiously patronize, pick, and purchase the choicest, plumpest produce from those renowned, green-thumbed, black-garbed gardeners retailing out of an old, yellow schoolbus that's been converted to a makeshift storefront.

No matter where we notice them or under what circumstances we engage them, Hutterites are not only a special and unique people but are, paradoxically, as contemporary as they are traditional. In this day and age, their survival and success depend on such an effective and skillful synthesis.

Their roots grew out of the Protestant Reformation and anchor the denominational foundation upon which Hutterian practices and priorities have been based for the last six centuries. Anabaptist in scope, Hutterites reject infant baptism, preferring instead to wait until an adult can consciously decide to make a personal profession of faith. Moreover, they advocate the total separation of church and state, as well as complete religious independence and free will. Besides being pacifists opposed to carrying guns, military service, and war, Hutterites promote their religio-, agri-communalism as the most heavenly way to reach their earthly goals.

Communes of the Hutterian Brethren dot the prairie provinces of Canada plus the Northern Plains of Montana, the Dakotas, Minnesota, Washington, and, soon, Oregon. Individual colonies may house as few as 50 or as many as 150 people. This communal way of life is founded on Biblical scripture and the teachings of Jesus Christ. Sam Hofer, head minister of the Surprise Creek Colony outside Stanford, Montana, proudly professes, "Our belief is based on Acts 2: 37–47 where everything is in common and everything's together. There is nothing mine nor thine. All belongs to the colony and the colony belongs to all."

Another Hutterian minister continues, "Hutterites live together for their religious beliefs. They came together under Jacob Hutter 560 years ago in the old country [Moravia]. We try to follow the Lord's footsteps as He taught us in the New Testament. We live together equally and share everything in common, as He would have us do. The colony gives you anything and everything you need. I have no money. All the money goes in one pot and everything is distributed equally." Tongue in cheek, Preacher Peter stipulates, "The only thing the colony might not provide us with is . . . a harmonica! I've always wanted a harmonica!"

Though Hutterites are virtually the same and rally under a single banner and basic belief system, three "branches" of Hutterianism exist to encompass the idiosyncratic differences between their original leaders. With *leut* meaning "people" in German, the *Dariusleuts*,

Lehrerleuts, and *Schmiedeleuts* are those who followed Darius, Lehrer, and Schmiede, respectively.

Simplifying the breakdown, one-third of Montana's forty-five Hutterite colonies are *Dariusleut* and are located in the east-central portion of the state. The remaining two-thirds are *Lehrerleut bruderhofs* (i.e. synonomous with colony) and are mostly found in west-central Montana. Historically, the *Schmiedeleuts* have chosen not to expand beyond the Canadian provinces and Minnesota. Together, 3,000 Hutterites call Montana home. All totaled, nearly 46,000 Hutterian brothers and sisters live in the United States and Canada.

Spiritually, Hutterites believe that mankind was created as an integral component of a complex, divinely conceived and orchestrated natural universe to worship the all-loving, all-powerful creator. They see human beings as selfish, weak, and sinful . . . and in desperate need of God's glory, guidance, grace, and gifts. By having faith in the Heavenly Father, accepting the Bible as His divinely inspired Word, and repenting to Him for their wrong-doings, Hutterites can be redeemed, renewed, and ultimately resurrected.

In their daily speech, Hutterites utilize an Austro-Bavarian dialect. At Sunday worship services and their daily prayer meetings, a High German is chanted by the minister from centuries-old, handwritten sermons that have changed very little over the decades. Eli Hofer, head minister of the North Harlem colony, justifies the repetitious use of original sermons: "There is really nothing new under the sun. We can still teach our people using sermons that were written in the 1600s because we have the same system and thought patterns."

Hutterian children learn English on a formal basis when they begin kindergarten at the colony grade school and continue until they complete the eighth grade. Simultaneously, the kids attend German language classes under the tutelage of one of their own elders.

Among themselves, Hutterites dress alike though minor differences exist between *Dariusleut, Lehrerleut,* and *Schmiedeleut* apparel. They are obviously distinguishable from the "English," as "outsiders" are called. In God's eyes, all people are created equal. Appearances should be no exception and neither should the width or breadth of one's wardrobe in the closet. Men wear black coats, black pants, black hats, black shoes or boots, and black suspenders. Only the shirt may not be black—but then again, it just might be. Men who are married sport beards and those who are still single continue to be clean-shaven.

Dariusleut women wear dark, muted, floor-length dresses that may be solid, brocade, or subtly (small) polka-dot. Officially, their heads, arms, and legs are supposed to be totally covered. A young girl's hair is braided in the front, frames her forehead, and then is drawn to the rear in a bun. A woman's hairdo is about the same except that the hair in front is rolled instead of braided. Most females do not cut their hair in their lifetime though some occasionally trim it. At all times in public, women keep their hair covered with black scarves; polka dots are the traditional scarf pattern, although some colonies allow designs to be painted.

The uniform dress code for colony residents establishes an expected standard of identity for Hutterian men and women. For those communal brothers and sisters, a norm of conformity minimizes individuality and maximizes the common good of the group by making everyone look the same. The code also negates false expectations. In addition, it prevents the spotlight from shining too brightly on a well-dressed, fashion-conscious dandy. As well, it narrows the expanse and variety of clothes that would otherwise need to be hand-sewn by the womenfolk.

Contrasted with clothing worn by members of the larger society, Hutterite attire is distinctively unique and blatantly identifiable. These differences underline their separateness and reinforce their desired, self-imposed isolation. They want the world to know that, not only by their dress, but also by their beliefs and communal lifestyle, they are indeed unlike the rest of the world. And they are proud of it.

Hutterites effectively blend the extremes of their contrasting secular world with the conservatism of their own spirituality. They do not hesitate to utilize a high-tech tool or technique if it will modernize their system or benefit the bottom line. In other words, if the item promotes performance, possesses power, or provides productivity, then its procurement should be pursued. If the colony does not profit from its use in a quantitative or commendable way, then it is not worth the time, energy, or expense. For example, a satellite-guided, Global Positioning System to perfect the optimal seeding of a field is a positive contribution; networking Diablo II game CDs between colony computers so that inter-*bruderhof* warfare can take place is not justified.

The political hierarchy of a colony begins with God at the top who is Lord over mankind. Then, the minister sets the stage and establishes the status quo for his flock of parishioners. Usually, an assistant preacher, the colony boss (or business manager), and other department heads (e.g. chicken man, dairy man, hog man, shop man, etc.) compose the colony's council of elders or board of directors. Even though a woman serves as the head cook, she does not sit on the council with the menfolk because in the Biblical chain of command, male is over female. Thereafter, elders are over the younger and parents, of course, reign supreme over children.

Hutterite colonies are incorporated in the same way businesses are. They pay taxes on county, state, and federal levels. In fact, colonies pay road taxes, property taxes, corporate taxes, and special taxes on their schools because they are public and on *bruderhof* land.

On an individual basis, Hutterites pay income taxes. They are citizens of the United States and, subsequently, must pay taxes as a requirement of their citizenship. However, in reality, since they receive no outright salary from the colony and garner so few wages for temporary or occasional jobs on the "outside," actual amounts paid are minimal.

In fact, with so little real money flowing into the billfolds and purses of Hutterites, virtually everyone has none of it. Hence, no uneven distribution of wealth exists that would provoke jealousies and coveting. A small allowance is given to members and families once per month at a colony. In addition, when they go to town, the business manager will give each one some spending money for incidentals and a meal at KFC or Pizza Hut.

In salaries (none), in appearance (the same), and according to *bruderhof* rules, regulations, and expected behaviors, the colony comes first and the individual last. A Hutterite's free will is stifled from birth through childhood to adulthood. A brother's or sister's entire life is characterized by denying self and refusing self-fulfillment in favor of deferring to the common good of the colony. Self-development is forsaken for colony enhancement. If something is good for a colony, the logic goes, then it has to be great for *everyone* in the colony.

A Hutterite community is not just a congregation of devout, everyday worshippers, but also an efficient company of skilled, devoted workers, actually a veritable machine itself. Most colonies are dependent on farming and ranching pursuits for their own consumption. Moreover, many raise cash crops that contribute to the economic viability and vitality of the *bruderhof*.

Some colonies raise wheat, barley and oats. Others make hay. Numerous colonies focus on the production of beef, pork and poultry (ducks, geese, chicken and turkey), while many are in the business of eggs, milk, lamb and wool. A few colonies have beehives and produce honey, and others sell fresh veggies out of their gardens. Several communes even create cabinetry, dressers, caskets, and other custom furniture commercially in their elaborate, well-equipped woodshops.

All are in the business of being good neighbors to farmers and ranchers who live nearby. If time and schedules permit, Hutterites are more than willing to pitch in and help out when manpower is needed for a big project like barn-raising, rounding-up and branding cattle, or shearing sheep. Annie Hofer, mother of Montana's youngest minister, Ed Hofer of Turner, projects current Hutterite friendliness: "We try to live as peacefully as we can. Life is too short! You have to be neighborly and that's it! We take care of each other and those around us."

Colonies also have an exemplary inventory of heavy-duty machines and equipment that can serve as a repair center for their neighbors' problems, as well as their own. A trip next door to the *bruderhof* can save a farmer or rancher a distracting, time-robbing, cash-draining trip to town. What better way to create good will, be a good neighbor, have good interaction, and do a good turn than to reach out, help someone in need, and contribute to a healthy, developing, maybe lifetime friendship.

As a photographer, writer, friend, and admirer of Hutterites for over twenty-five years, I have been blessed with the honor, joy and privilege of visiting many Montana colonies. I have seen firsthand how gracious, humble, true and caring these uncomplicated people of deep faith are. They communicate with blunt honesty, they love with open hearts, and they give with genuine warmth and hospitality. In fact, a more generous people I have yet to meet!

However, not all people have the time, reason, opportunity, or means to travel to a Hutterian *bruderhofs*. Hutterites deserve to be seen in their own environment, through their eyes and perspectives, distilled through their values and beliefs if they are to be recognized and truly known for who they really are.

For those who cannot visit a colony, the next best thing can be found in this book. For a culture that has remained rather closed, a door is opening. For a system that has traditionally met outside opinions with silence, a Hutterite voice is speaking. Out of the shadows of an unknown people who dress and live differently, a gentle, human face is visible, has opened the door to Hutterite life, and is welcoming outsiders in.

She is real. She smiles. She speaks and writes. She gives of herself. Of her family. Of her Hutterian community. Lisa Marie Stahl, the young Hutterite woman from the Gildford Colony on Montana's Hi-Line, has done more to share her culture through her newspaper columns than anyone could have imagined five years ago when she first began.

With her pen, she has clarified issues of importance. Instead of having to turn the other cheek, she has struck down rumors that propagate misconceptions and repulsed fallacies that breed prejudice. With her keyboard, she has spread cultural understanding, greater acceptance, and brotherly/sisterly love. Through her eyes, then her words, she has yielded a clear vision of the special, spiritual, communal world of Hutterites, rare among today's cultures of the world where sacred meaning, community fulfillment, and the value of human life are conspicuously absent.

Unfortunately, the regular issuance of new columns by Lisa Marie Stahl has come to a close. She has matured beyond her twenty young years, chosen baptism and marriage, and opted for God, husband, and family. That does not imply that her words necessarily go silent or her sentiments grow cold. It merely means that you hold onto this volume of collected essays until you see a new byline from Canada by Lisa Marie Tschetter!

Introducing Lisa

‿◟◝◟◝◞

by Karen Ogden,
Great Falls Tribune regional editor

December 26, 1999

Except for the closet full of homemade dresses, Lisa Marie Stahl's bedroom could belong to any seventeen-year-old girl, anywhere in America. Glow-in-the-dark stars dangle from the ceiling by bits of string. Teen idols strike two-dimensional poses on the walls. Her most adored possessions, a collection of glass and porcelain figurines, are carefully arranged on the dressertop beneath snapshots of friends stuck to the mirror.

"Don't come between a girl and her diary. You'll be tomorrow's topic," warns a computer printout on one wall.

In this private room, Lisa sits down at her word processor each week and gives Montanans a rare, public glimpse of life at the Gildford Hutterite Colony thirty miles west of Havre. For two years her column has been a Friday fixture in the *Havre Daily News*, drawing a pile of fan mail from as far away as Washington State. Her column will run monthly in the *Great Falls Tribune* starting January 2.

Lisa has tackled the topics of death, pesky little sisters, Down's syndrome, Halloween, butcher week and scores of other issues culled from the rhythm of her daily life. What Lisa hasn't written about is the next century and what it holds for a young Hutterite woman with a deep devotion to God and her culture, a love of sewing, a dream of travel and a knack for journalism.

"The future can come by itself," Lisa said, enjoying cookies and juice with a guest at her kitchen table. "It comes fast enough."

Just Another Day

Lisa, like the majority of people on Montana's forty-five Hutterite Colonies, is living for the present and keeping alive the traditions of her people's past. The new millennium won't get so much as a toot on a noisemaker come January 1, 2000.

"We could get together and have a party, but I don't see much sense in it," Lisa said.

Sitting at her family's kitchen table, Lisa's appearance is as straightforward and matter-of-fact as her personality. She wears a plain, plaid dress and sturdy black shoes. Her chestnut-colored hair is carefully rolled back into a black-and-white polka-dot headscarf, which is mandatory for women in her colony.

"[New Year's] is not really that important in my society," Lisa said. "I don't think it's that important to go out and get drunk about. It's just another day."

Contrary to the stereotype, Lisa's outspokenness isn't unusual, said Jim Gretch, a Great Falls, Montana, resident who has spent years studying and visiting with the Hutterites. "When you get to know a [Hutterite] family close enough, it's not unusual to meet a young woman who's outspoken and has a strong personality," Gretch said.

But it is rare for a Hutterite woman to express her thoughts publicly as Lisa has, especially in a daily newspaper.

Hutterites are not secretive about their austere, communal lifestyle. Anyone is free, in fact welcome, to visit the colonies. Yet given the Hutterite's history of persecution—they fled Russia in the 1870s to escape religious oppression—and their emphasis on modesty, they rarely seek publicity.

A Little Help

Lisa got her start when she asked the teacher at her colony's school to organize a class tour at the *Havre Daily News*. Already the publisher of her school paper, the *Gildford Colony Gazette*, Lisa wanted to meet a "real" reporter.

"I just wanted a little help from somebody," Lisa said. "I didn't have anybody to teach me journalism."

The reporter Lisa met was Kathy Lundman, who remembered reading an essay Lisa wrote about Hutterite weddings that was on display at the Great Northern Fair. On the spot, she invited Lisa to write a column.

Lisa's mom, Susanna, quickly warmed to the idea. "I knew she had a real interest in writing and it was a good opportunity for her so I just let her go ahead and do it," she said.

But Lisa's grandfather was reticent. As the colony's minister, the most important man in the social hierarchy, he is responsible for the colony's moral integrity. His decisions weigh heavily on the colony's future.

"It was never done," Lisa said. "Nobody ever heard of a Hutterite columnist."

Her grandfather agreed to the column on one condition.

"He just told me that if it interferes with the colony, I'd have to quit," Lisa said. Lisa's mother would be her editor.

Down to Earth

Not everyone in the Hutterite community approves of Lisa's work, and Susanna Stahl has heard about it.

But the feedback, both on and off the colonies, is overwhelmingly positive. Lisa has introduced readers to her Uncle Joe, who has Down's syndrome and a special place in the hearts of his family.

When Sam Stahl, Lisa's cousin and a well-liked man both on and off the colony, was killed in a truck accident last September, Lisa chronicled the colony's preparations leading up to the funeral.

Most often, her columns capture the joys of everyday life and work, be it feather plucking, soap-making or babysitting. Lisa is one of seven children, including three little sisters.

"I never miss reading her articles," said Big Sandy farmer Ruth Pegar. "It's just down to Earth. She's kind of like 'the way it is' from butchering chickens to everything."

Harriet Stenwick follows Lisa's columns all the way from Poulsbo, Washington. Stenwick grew up in Kremlin, just ten miles east of Gildford, and her sister Janet Sorenson still lives there. Though she winters in Arizona, Sorenson faithfully clips and mails the column to her sister each week during the summer.

Through Lisa's eyes, Stenwick remembers her own experiences on the farm.

"The one time that she wrote about when they were butchering geese, I got such a kick out of it," Stenwick said.

Lisa finds inspiration in an adage taped above her word processor.

"Reporters are born, not made," it says.

But she can't expect to write forever, at least not in a daily newspaper. Lisa's colony is comprised of about twelve families and she's related, by blood or marriage, to just about everyone.

"When I get married I'll move to another colony, another state or maybe even another country," Lisa said, surrounded by the familiarity of her family's warm, wood-paneled kitchen. Most Hutterite colonies are in Canada.

Montana has two types of Hutterite colonies, Lehrerleut and Dariusleut, which lead slightly different lifestyles. Lisa's colony is the latter and the more liberal. Unlike the Lehrerleut, Dariusleut families can use microwaves in their homes. Dariusleut weddings are larger and more festive, and girls and boys are permitted to play sports such as baseball together.

Gildford is particularly liberal, Lisa said.

But the elders at her future husband's colony, wherever that may be, might not accept her writing, much less her other ambitions.

"Maybe things will be different there," Lisa said.

Lisa is under no pressure to get married. Some Hutterites never do.

"It's a big step, marriage," Lisa said. "Something I'm too young to think of right now."

Lisa graduated from high school last year. Her first step into adulthood will be baptism, which is required for marriage.

The Hutterites are "Anabaptist" Christians, meaning they are baptized only as adults, usually after the age of twenty, when they can make an educated and conscious decision to devote their lives to God.

Some, especially young men, aren't baptized until they're well into their thirties.

God and Sacrifice

Hutterite baptism is not only a pledge to God, Gretch said, but also a commitment to the Hutterite's austere, communal way of life, with all of its advantages and sacrifices.

"That's a decision that every individual has to make when they come to a point in their life when they commit to baptism," Gretch said. "They are exposed enough to the outside world when they come to town that they know what they're giving up."

Lisa's life will revolve around kitchen duty, housework, church, soap-making, harvest, seeding, weeding, babysitting, mending—all depending on the time of day and the season.

She will never have a career outside her colony. Because a Hutterite colony's income is communal, Lisa will never have her own savings account.

She will never go to college or take a backpacking trip through Europe.

"I've always wanted to travel to different states, to different countries. I know that will never happen," Lisa said. "I've always wanted to see an ocean."

To a young woman "out in the world"—as Hutterites refer to society outside the colonies—such limits could be unbearable. To Lisa, they are expected and accepted.

"It just doesn't happen every day that you get what you want," she says.

Don't Play Games

But Lisa also will never worry about mortgage payments. When Lisa marries, her husband's colony will build or provide a furnished home. On this afternoon, in a nearby house, a spirited group of young men and women is upholstering a new couch for a couple who will be married the next weekend.

Lisa will never pay for a babysitter, or fret about finding a good one, because the other colony women will help. She won't have to save for retirement or live in a nursing home.

Nor will Lisa worry about insurance policies, wills, elder care or the other headaches of life in the twenty-first century.

Lisa said she will be baptized one day. But she's waiting until she's good and ready.

"You don't want to play games with God," she said. "You want to do it once and you want to be serious about it."

Until then, Lisa's in the gray area, which, according to Gretch, the Hutterites sometimes refer to as the "wild years." Compared to many young women her age, Lisa's life is anything but wild.

But being seventeen, she likes to test the boundaries a little.

That Dress

Sewing is a good avenue.

"I can't think of anything I love as much as sewing," Lisa says, opening a closet full of homemade dresses.

Most are in line with her colony's traditional style—hair smoothed back into a black-and-white polka-dot scarf paired with a plain, ankle-length dress most often in plaid or a floral print.

But Lisa's favorite is a modest, two-piece burgundy satin dress. Its debut provoked a universal family scene. "My dad said, 'Where did you get that dress?'" Lisa recalled, laughing.

It used to be satin was only for brides, but now fashionable young Hutterite women wear it as wedding guests too, she explains. Young women in some colonies also wear slip-on shoes, unlike their mothers who stick to more conservative lace-ups.

In addition to clothing, Lisa makes computer-designed wedding invitations as a hobby and for a little extra pocket change. She loves baseball and Western-themed Christian romance novels.

On summer evenings, Lisa often gets one of her three brothers to show her how to operate the combines.

For the Hutterites

Yet most of Lisa's time is spent learning to cook, sew, make soap and the other skills she'll need as an adult in the colony—the fodder for her column.

"[The column is] so positive because it cuts a lot of barriers," said Lisa's former high school teacher Darcy Zook. "People outside the colony don't look at Hutterites as being human sometimes . . . I think her column has really helped. It's opened doors and people can understand why they do things this way."

Lisa said it's her fan mail, both positive and negative, that reminds her she's making a difference. "It made me realize how important my writing as a hobby is for me," Lisa said. "I can stick up for myself—not only myself, but for the community, for the Hutterites."

Lisa Marie Stahl holds up the three dresses she made to wear
for her shivarees and wedding ceremony.

Introduction

⊱✦⊰

I was fourteen years old when I was first introduced to the world of journalism. Our schoolteacher at the colony asked the class if we'd like to start a colony/school newspaper.

Of course the answer was, "No, Hutterites don't write newspapers. There are no Hutterite reporters."

It turned out that I was in for a surprise. Not only did God grant me the gift of writing, but I ended up becoming the publisher of the *Gildford Colony Gazette*.

The following spring, our teacher arranged a tour of the *Havre Daily News* offices. The tour left me anxious to talk with a "real reporter," so I asked if there was anyone willing to chat with me. One of the newspaper's part-time reporters, Kathy Lundman, spared a few minutes of her day with me. She soon learned that I wasn't just there for the tour, and after much pondering, she asked, "Would you happen to be the girl who wrote a short story about a Hutterite wedding, that I saw at the fair last summer?"

I blushed at the recognition, and the rest of the class buzzed with excitement as they exchanged looks and smiles. Kathy told me that sometimes people write for the paper as "stringer reporters."

I was interested, but at the time I thought the opportunity was pointless because I'd need the colony's permission, and I didn't expect to get it.

I WAS granted permission and started my first column, naive and unaware of what would be in store for me in the future. My mom edited all my articles before I faxed them to the newspaper.

Almost two years later, another opportunity knocked at my door. My column had caught the attention of Karen Ogden, regional editor at the *Great Falls Tribune,* who invited me to write for the paper. My area of topics was much larger at the *Tribune* because I'd have brainstorming sessions with my editor and other staff writers on trips to Great Falls and over the phone.

I wrote my column, called "On the Colony", for three years before I decided to give it up forever. I had other priorities: to be baptized into the Hutterite faith and dedicate my future to God, the One I owe all my thanks for all the blessings in my life, and to dedicate my life to my future husband and family. It was a difficult decision I made myself, though it disappointed some people, especially my immediate family. But I felt that after five years of writing, God was calling me to step into another phase in my life. My future was in His hands, and I was sure He'd still have many special plans in store for me.

I grew up on a Hutterite colony in north-central Montana called Gildford Colony, where I lived until several weeks shy of my twenty-first birthday. In the summer of 2003, I married and moved to Saskatchewan, Canada, where I joined my husband's colony.

I come from a family of nine. I lost my father less than a month after celebrating my first birthday. He died when he was overcome by fumes while cleaning out the pits at the colony's pig barns on July 30, 1983. He left behind four children, my three older brothers and me.

Five years later, on May 29, 1988, my mother remarried, and in the next few years, God blessed me with three sisters who I love and cherish dearly. Many times I took the opportunity to write about their experiences on the colony, and they loved having their names mentioned in my column.

Growing up on the colony, I always wondered about the Hutterite lifestyle. Though I occasionally was nervous and angry at the stares and questions of strangers visiting the colony and in town, I came to respect my culture. I often looked for opportunities to share with the public why we dress differently and why we choose to live communally. Though at times people questioned aspects of my column, I believe God opened enough doors to change the understanding of the general public toward my society.

The Hutterites came to North America on July 5, 1874, from Russia. They made the decision to leave Europe after years of persecution and having to flee from one country to another. Upon their arrival in America, the group was split into three sects: the Lehrerleut, Dariusleut, and Schmiedeleut. My colony is Dariusleut, and all the information in my column is about the Dariusleut, unless otherwise stated.

My biggest goal while writing was to share my culture's tradition and allow my column to become a learning tool for non-Hutterites. I hope I've brought a better understanding to our "English" neighbors who were many times too shy to ask, "Why?"

Life as a Hutterite

⤷⊙⊙⤶

On the Colony

I'd like to welcome you to join me as I inform you about a group's culture that so often keeps people puzzled about their ways, wondering about their traditions and intrigued enough to want to learn more.

The Hutterian Brethren became a part of Montana when the first colony settled in the state in 1912. They've since expanded to about forty-five colonies. Though there are three groups of Hutterites, only two reside in Montana—the Lehrerleut and Dariusleut. I'm Dariusleut.

Most of the Dariusleut colonies in Montana are originally from Canada. There are only a few that came from colonies in South Dakota. My own colony branched away from a colony around Lewistown. It's been in existence for almost thirty years.

My immediate family consists of nine members. I have three brothers who are older and three sisters who are younger. Together with my parents, I have a very close-knit family. Each of them are very supportive of my ambition to write columns about the Hutterites for a public newspaper, and it's their continuous support that's my encouragement.

I discovered my love of working with words around the age of fourteen, although at the time journalism was the furthest from my mind. It's not that I couldn't picture myself as a journalist; I just thought I wouldn't know how to write a news story. But when my teacher suggested our colony school start a newspaper, I gave it a try and almost immediately discovered how much I liked it.

That school year, the *Gildford Colony Gazette* developed and I got my first whiff of journalism. Several months later, and after a class tour of the *Havre Daily News*, I was writing my first column for a local public newspaper. I couldn't believe it—fifteen years old, and I had my own column.

For almost two years, I wrote weekly columns in the *Havre Daily News* informing the people of Havre about my culture. I can't express enough how much I enjoyed the experience. My ideas were never rejected, and I could write from my heart. I also was respected for my ideas and my enthusiasm.

When I was invited to write a monthly column for the *Great Falls Tribune*, I couldn't believe my luck. Now I had such a big opportunity to reach and inform so many more people about the culture and traditions of the Hutterites.

My goal in writing a column has always been to tell people who the Hutterites are and why they live by such standards. My goal is to clear up any misunderstandings and to have you see our world through the eyes of a teenage Hutterite girl. I want to share with you the joys and advantages of choosing to live in a colony and why I'd never desire to live anywhere else.

I'm finally doing what I've always dreamed of. But I'm also curious to learn what my readers would like to read about each month.

I have a distant dream to see more colony youths become involved in journalism, even if only in the way I started out—by writing in a colony/school newspaper. I'd like to encourage them not to be scared to express themselves publicly and to always be proud of their heritage.

And as far as I see things, no one could do the job better than someone who was brought up as a Hutterite and knows firsthand what life is like living in and being part of a colony.

Hutterite Culture
Revolves around Church

The Hutterite church is the foundation of my culture's style of communal living. Events taking place there set a person's life goals and prepare them for whatever their future might hold.

The church's design is simple—there are benches on both sides of the aisle, sometimes wooden, sometimes cushioned. At the front of the church to the left, there is a bench where the elders of the colony sit—the financial boss, field boss and German schoolteacher.

To the right of the bench, front and center, is the minister's desk where two ministers sit.

In old Hutterite tradition, the men sit on the left side of the church while the women sit on the right.

They all sit according to their age, with the oldest in the back and the youngest in the front. There is never confusion because all of us know our appointed seats.

Hutterite churches are not decorated with pictures, candles, fancy windows or a cross at the front because the Hutterite faith sees these things as distractions.

There are no pianos or other musical instruments in Hutterite churches. All the singing is done a cappella, with one of the ministers leading the song. All the songs are written in High German as well as all the sermons. During church, one minister will lead the song while the other minister officiates.

When a new colony starts out, building the church is just as important as anything else built on the colony. Even if at first there won't be an actual building for church, there will always be an alternate place to hold the services until there is. Sometimes the alternate is the kitchen's dining area.

In newer colonies, the church is usually connected to the communal kitchen. Sometimes, as in older colonies, the church will

Currently the youngest Hutterite preacher in Montana,
Eddie Hofer wears the classic minister attire.

stand alone, as is the case at our colony. Many colonies with church buildings large enough to hold several hundred people also have their funerals at the church.

The colony elders and Brothers (the baptized colony men) also use the church for council meetings. At Christmastime the children set up and perform their Christmas program at the church. Spring graduations are also held there.

But most importantly, every Sunday morning at nine o'clock, the Sunday service begins. Those attending go willingly, as no one is forced to attend. (If a person is sick and not feeling very well, he or she can be excused.)

The ministers do not get paid for the service. Their work is a service to the community.

The church also is home to a prayer service at 5:30 each evening. We call this service "gebet" or Evening Prayer.

From age five, young Hutterite students attend two classes of German school daily. The classes are taught at the church with the students' desks set up in front of the pews. The German school-teacher, a man from the colony appointed for the job, uses the "minister's table" as a teacher's desk.

Sunday school classes are held Sunday afternoon following the noon meal. All school-age children and all unbaptized adults attend the classes.

Sometime between the ages of nineteen and twenty-six—after attending seven weeks of baptism classes—young colony members are baptized at the church with the entire congregation attending.

Later, when they make the decision to marry, another life event takes place at the colony church.

New Colonies Take Time, Patience to Build

When a colony becomes too large to provide both homes and enough work for all of its members, it must branch out and form a sister colony. It takes years of planning, building and developing to complete (or even partially complete) a new colony.

My colony, the Gildford Colony on the Hi-Line west of Havre, was bought and established in 1971. We now total fifty-five people. We are named after the nearby town of Gildford. We branched from the Deerfield Colony near Danvers northwest of Lewistown.

At the start, several of the men went to live on the new place to get things established. Three or four of the ladies later joined them to cook and tidy up their temporary living facilities.

For more than three years they boarded in a two-story house already on the new colony grounds. First they built a pig barn so the colony would have a source of income while building. In 1974, they added two four-unit homes and a communal kitchen, which at the time was used to can vegetables, wash clothes and butcher.

During this time, an old granary already on the colony was used for a chicken barn. There also was an old barn, part of which was used to milk five cows. The other part was used as a communal laundry room until the kitchen was built.

Five families moved to the Gildford Colony in December 1974, a total of thirty-three people. After the homes were built, the two-story home was converted into a school and carpentry shop.

In the winter of 1975, shortly after New Year's, a colony lady was elected to teach the ten children for the remainder of the school year. The following school year, the teacher from the colony we branched away from joined my colony to stay on as our schoolteacher. She taught for several years and helped establish our own public school. In 1977, we got our own district.

In 1975, the church was built; it also served as a German and English school.

There also was a small mechanic shop, which my colony used as a garage in the early years. Unfortunately, it burned to the ground early one morning in September 1976. The cause of the fire was never determined. That day we lost the entire shop and work tools, along with a tractor that was in the shop for repairs. We replaced the shop the next spring.

In 1980 we added another pig barn. Three years later our milking barn and carpentry shop were built, and we added a horse barn in 1984.

Eleven years later, in 1995, my colony built a brand new kitchen. Today, the old kitchen is used for canning and as a slaughterhouse.

In the late 1970s, while most of the building was going on, my colony was very short-handed so our neighbors came to help us out. They included colonies belonging to my Hutterite group, the Dariusleut, and the more conservative Lehrerleut.

They gave us a big hand, helping us with most of the barns and also shingling and siding the houses. We were grateful for their help, because we couldn't have done it without them. The work was done voluntarily, like a barn-raising in an Amish community.

Because we were so short-handed, the young school-aged boys and girls had to take on adult responsibilities and help out with the colony chores and building. In a way, they changed from childhood into adulthood at a young age.

My grandparents have fond memories of those early years, when they delivered fresh cream and eggs to the surrounding neighbors. They had their steady customers along the Hi-Line. The people in town always knew which days to expect them, so they made sure they had their empty jars ready to return. Customers who wouldn't be home that day left a note on their front door specifying how much cream and how many eggs they wanted. The door was unlocked and on the kitchen table were the empty cream jars from the previous week with enough money inside to pay for that day's order.

With the money from the weekly egg and cream runs, my grandparents were able to pay for the entire colony's groceries.

Unlike today, the land carried good crops in the 1970s, and wheat prices were high. So even though the start of the new colony was laborious, the land was promising, giving us a chance to provide and furnish all the needs of our newly established Hutterite community.

Familiarity, Comfort of Weekends on Colony Make Them a Favorite

As a young child growing up on the colony, my favorite part of the week was always the weekend. Today it still is.

What I loved most about it as a child was there was no school on the weekend. If we brought home any homework, we could put it off until late Sunday night. We had a German school class Saturday morning, but it only lasted until ten. We'd spend the rest of the day playing with our friends until our mothers called us home in the late afternoon.

These days, my Saturdays usually start off with a light breakfast of cereal at the communal kitchen, where everybody meets at seven o'clock for breakfast. The ladies bake fresh buns on Saturday, so everyone looks forward to dropping in at the kitchen's bakery around nine o'clock for a sample.

During the winter months, we have a lunch of fresh buns, Saturday sausage and gasha (potato and onion soup). We normally make the Saturday sausage around Thanksgiving to last us through the winter months. Though the meal is very simple to prepare, it still tends to be everyone's favorite.

On Saturday afternoons, we normally take a bath and dress in our Sunday church clothes (special weekend clothes) and everyone is dressed up at that evening's prayer meeting and supper. The ladies will wear a new dress they recently made themselves, usually crepe or rayon. The men like to dress in crisp white shirts and dress pants.

Supper Saturday is usually a big meal of either stuffed chicken, cut-up geese or beef stew. Saturday is also when the cooks make their big dessert for the week. Usually they save their new dessert recipes for that day or they'll make an old favorite.

After the supper dishes are washed and everyone has gone home to be with their families, each family will pass around High German songbooks and sing several German songs together. This is my favorite part of the weekend. It's one of the rare times during the week that my whole family gets together to spend some family time.

After we've sung, we'll share with our family what we did that week, perhaps a lesson learned at work, and talk about our plans for the coming week. We'll share a few laughs, and soon our sitting room will start to fill with some of our colony neighbors. During the summer months, some of the families go for walks around our farm together after supper.

We usually retire late, but not too late, so we can attend breakfast at seven on Sunday morning. We serve breakfast the same time every morning, and only on special occasions, like weddings, do we sleep in.

Sunday mornings are quiet and peaceful. After doing some light house tidying, my family will join together for a German morning song, usually one everyone knows by heart. Just before nine, we'll prepare to attend that morning's church sermon.

For church, the ladies wear a black church jacket with long sleeves. The men also wear black church jackets. All the men wear the same style jacket, except for the ministers. They wear a minister's jacket that reaches to their knees and is parted in the back up to the waist.

Church lasts for an hour and twenty minutes. The colony members attend church, except for the cooks who are excused to prepare lunch. The school-age children take turns staying home from church to babysit their younger brothers and sisters.

Lunch follows church at 10:30. Normally on Sunday, we'll serve roasted ducks and noodle soup. Once in a while, we'll have roasted chicken with grits soup.

At 1:30, all the unbaptized members of the colony and the children who attend school will attend a class of Sunday school, taught by the German schoolteacher. At Sunday school, each student will recite a small quotation he or she heard at church that morning. The German schoolteacher will explain the quotation's definition in depth, speaking the German that we speak in our homes. We also read several passages from the New Testament in German and the adult students (fifteen and older) who no longer attend German school will recite a German song that they learned during the week.

After Sunday school lets out, everyone slowly wanders home to do something quiet—take a nap, read a book or go for a walk.

Sundays, we have our evening prayer meeting at five o'clock instead of 5:30. Supper follows at 5:30. The rest of the evening is spent with the family or visiting friends.

After a busy week, everyone looks forward to the weekend. It's a reserved time to spend with God, our family and reading the Bible, for we must not lose our connection with any of these.

First Day of Classes Makes Life a Bit Easier for Everyone

Monday, school officially starts at the Gildford Colony School. What a blessing!

It's not a day too early, either. It'll put a smile on everyone's face when they see the kids heading back to school.

It'll take a burden off the guys who work around the shop and barns with big equipment, since they constantly have to be on the watch for kids at play.

It'll bring a sigh of relief to the moms, too. They're tired of breaking up fights and repeating chores that should have been done two hours before playtime began. No more looking for my sisters who sneaked out of the house before they finished doing their chores (like I wouldn't notice).

For the past three weeks, the school kids have been extra hyper, I think, to make the best of their last few days of summer vacation. They seem to sense that summer is coming to an end, and they're sure letting us know about it.

Shortly after English school classes start for the year, their German classes will follow. The kids will be taught to read and write in German for forty-five minutes in the morning and an hour in the afternoon.

They're eager to meet their new teacher—almost as much as the parents are.

The 2000–01 school year will consist of eight students, ranging from three first-graders to a high schooler. They attend a public school on the colony grounds, taught by a certified teacher from town.

High school is attended at the colony via correspondence courses. This has been in effect for the past ten-plus years.

Colony parents have a lot of say in their children's education, since the school board consists of only colony members. This job is open to both moms and dads.

I personally feel that attending a small colony school is an opportunity, though there are a few disadvantages.

The students never get to ride a public bus with other kids. They don't have a gym or a cafeteria, and they don't have lockers.

But there are advantages to some of these things.

There is no need for a bus because the school is a few yards from their homes. Our sports and PE activities are all done outside on the playground, close to nature. There is no need for a cafeteria because the kids eat lunch with the rest of the colony. Besides, who would turn down a home-cooked meal?

Lockers aren't needed because each of us has our own personal desk where we store all our books and accessories. We don't need to worry about carrying around books all day because all classes are in the same classroom.

Hall rush-hour madness is never a problem.

I have a special place in my heart for teachers. Parents have a lot to be thankful for. Teachers take on the responsibility of teaching other people's children to read and write, about sharing and caring and discipline. They play an important role in society.

I have to admit, teachers have class!

Teacher Provides Vital Link to Colony

A Hutterite English teacher provides and fulfills a unique need within a Hutterite colony. She is a link for our school children, connecting them with the world beyond the colony grounds and educating them for whatever their future might hold—whether they'll someday be a colony boss, a minister or even the head cook.

Sarita Kuhn, the English teacher at our colony, lives in Havre. The distance doesn't bother her because she likes her job so much. Each day she says that she discovers something new about the kids she teaches, the colony and the people living there. I recently spent an afternoon talking with Mrs. Kuhn about her experience teaching on the colony.

Her normal workdays start at about five in the morning. She enjoys the hour's drive to work because it gives her a chance to plan her day and spend some time by herself.

Even though Mrs. Kuhn likes to keep in touch with the students' parents with notes, she also likes to interact with the other people on our colony in ways that include everyone in the students' school lives. She especially likes to include the ladies because they have more available time than the men.

This fall, just before school was ready to start, she invited all the colony members to an open house celebration at the school. She took everyone on a tour of the building, showing the changes that were made after the school was remodeled this summer. To show her appreciation for all the work the colony members had done, Mrs. Kuhn personally made curtains to liven up the classroom.

Her involvement doesn't end there. At the recent annual geese butchering, Mrs. Kuhn turned the event into a morning social studies project. The lesson was to teach the children what being part of a community is all about. They had to volunteer their help at butchering, from jobs like babysitting to helping clean the geese. To do her part of the community service project, our teacher babysat the kindergarten students and some younger that morning.

Our German vocabulary seems to be the most challenging thing for all of our teachers. As a result, "Do not speak German at school" tends to be the No. 1 rule for every teacher. Although there is a language barrier, Mrs. Kuhn says her students speak very fluent English because over the past decade more and more English is being spoken in the homes. Because of this, most of her kindergarten students speak very good English when they start school, and only occasionally does she need an older student to translate for her.

Our teacher likes our dress code. In fact, Mrs. Kuhn says that because of it, she feels there is little peer pressure among the students. The colony kids are always playing or working together. In some situations they actually try to eliminate peer pressure. For example, at the annual Christmas program, all the schoolgirls would pick a color of dress to wear that night. Out of respect for each other, they'd decide on wearing one dress that all the girls would have. This way, no one would feel out of place.

Through the students, Mrs. Kuhn can usually tell what's happening on the colony. She knows what fruit the colony gets or what was baked that week because the kids are always bringing her snacks and treats. Her favorites are the pastries and buns.

Occasionally, she'll even join them for lunch, but usually she prefers to stay at school to correct papers and get caught up with how the kids are doing on their schoolwork. Once in a while, if there's a favorite meal planned for lunch or the cooks are trying out a new recipe, the teacher will get a personal invitation to attend lunch that day.

Our teacher says the children are very fortunate to be living in a colony. They always have both their parents around, and they have an extended family as well. The bond is especially great with grandparents. There is always someone there to look out for their needs. When a parent is away or at work or on vacation, an aunt, uncle or grandparent will be there to look after the children, so they are never left with total strangers. Another advantage is learning more than one language. The students stay fluent their whole lives. Mrs. Kuhn especially admires the support system. She thinks it's wonderful to do big jobs together such as canning and gardening because it's much more fun that way than doing it alone.

Mrs. Kuhn has many prized memories from teaching at Hutterite colonies. She previously taught school at the East End Colony north of Havre. This is her second year teaching at our colony.

"When any of my students have a new baby born in their family, I will give them a present for the baby," Mrs. Kuhn said. "The students are always excited because I put a lot of curling ribbon on the packages, and they look pretty. When the students return to school, they bring me a gift from home of canned cherries, a grapefruit, candy or other food."

Mrs. Kuhn often feels as though she's the one who got the gift, she said.

"The students and families at the colonies where I have taught are very appreciative of every little thing I did for the students or them," she said. "They show their appreciation for things that I would never get a 'thank you' for from anyone outside the colony."

A Day in the Life of a Hutterite Child
Similar to Those Outside Colony

The clock on our kitchen wall reads 6:50. For the second time, I walk into the room my three sisters share to wake them. Several minutes later, standing in line in the bathroom waiting to do her hair, my sister Gloria, age ten, asks me, "Why didn't you wake us? We're gonna be late for breakfast."

"I did," I answer. "You just kept pushing my snooze button, just like you do your alarm's."

So starts a typical Hutterite child's day, as the lights come on in homes throughout the colony.

Minutes later, the girls grab their jackets and hurry out the door just as breakfast is announced over the pager. They sprint off for a day that's mixed with lessons in our traditional High German language, along with English lessons—bringing them into contact with the world beyond the boundaries of a Hutterite colony.

They share a hearty breakfast of bacon, eggs and toast with the rest of the children on the colony. Eating in a dining room separate from the adults, the children are under close supervision by the German schoolteacher and his wife. They sit according to their age, with boys separate from the girls, just as the adults sit in a separate dining room. When they finish their meal, they go about washing their breakfast dishes and setting the table for the lunch meal. By 7:30, they're heading across the yard to the communal church, where they'll attend forty-five minutes of German school.

During their German classes, the students are being taught to read, write and understand High German, since it is not spoken fluently in our homes.

This morning, after singing a German song together and saying their morning prayers, they recite several rhyming verses the German schoolteacher assigned them to learn the night before. The students attend German school from the time they are five to fifteen. German school lets out at 8:15, giving the students fifteen minutes to prepare for English school, taught in another building.

During this past summer, my colony remodeled the English school. The men made several convenient changes so there would be more room and the building would be more organized. They added a handicapped-accessible bathroom, a computer center and a conference room. They also divided the main classroom into sectional areas so the teacher could have three distinct classroom areas.

The students' day starts like a day in any other public classroom, and their curriculum follows state standards. They are taught the usual class subjects: math, reading, spelling, science, geography, health, etc.

They sit according to their grade levels, with fifth grade to high school on one end, first to fourth in the middle and kindergarten at the end. Our school consists of thirteen students and is taught by one teacher. The students do a lot of textbook work.

Our teacher has many exciting projects planned for the students this school year. One that is way at the top of the students' interest list is getting an ant farm. She's also working on teaching them word-processing, spreadsheets and how to use databases. Another exciting project is writing and publishing a book with the students. Each chapter in the book will include one story on colony life written by each student.

The students' classes end at 3:30 in the afternoon. They go home for an after-school snack before attending another German school class from four to five o'clock. At 5:30, all the families attend a twenty-minute prayer meeting at the communal church, with supper following at six.

After supper, the kids join together for a game of hide and seek or tag—IF they don't have any chores to do at home. The chores for the children on the colony are chosen for them according to their gender. Girls will help out at home, doing dishes, babysitting and general housecleaning. Boys will work with their fathers at the barn or mechanic shop. Some of the younger boys will help with the milking and feeding the other animals.

Around 7:30, as it starts getting dark, the children slowly venture home to do their German homework and spend some time with their families.

My sisters share their day with us, telling us about what happened

Joyce Stahl climbs the barn door gate at Surprise Creek Colony.

Anna Rose Hofer scores a point after a ball is dropped, and just about breaks her leg in the process.

at school, the good grade they got in reading or math and how an older sibling squealed their hiding place while playing hide and seek that evening.

Colony Youth Stay Busy with Hobbies, Games, Social Get-togethers

So many times people have asked me: "What do people do on the colony for hobbies, sports and entertainment?"

The list is endless. It varies from gender to age, to the season, occasion and weather.

With the men, it's the basic "all-male interests" that most non-Hutterites share. At the top of the list comes the usual—fishing. Next you'll find tractors, trucks and pickups. It's a male requirement to know the latest equipment available in ranching, the new device that was added to John Deere steering controls or the latest fish tackle.

In the summer months, on a lazy evening when all colony work has been excused for the day, the younger guys will start a volleyball or baseball game. Soon the single girls and school-aged kids will hear the commotion and join the game.

If the colony gets visitors (single guys and girls) they will be invited for a match of volleyball, usually our team against the visitors.

Later, as the evening goes on, the young folks will have a gathering at the shop or kitchen to socialize and get to know each other. (This is how most young Hutterites meet.) They'll sing hymns and play old favorite colony games such as "Upset the Fruit Basket," "Confusion," "Walk the White Line," and "Desert."

When a girl or boy turns fifteen (adult colony age) they are permitted to join the gatherings.

Young Hutterite girls can always find things to do, no matter what the season. During the winter months, they'll get sewing lessons from their mothers or older sisters.

Old trades will be passed on, like teaching the younger generation to knit, crochet and cross-stitch. Many young girls take an interest in making wheat weaving wall hangings, embroidering signs and even drawing and painting. Other girls find that their world revolves around reading books.

Some of my friends enjoy collecting teddy bears, stamps and comic books.

A personal favorite is collecting the work of Kim Anderson, famous for his nostalgic photographs of children in old-fashioned oversize clothes. I am also a big fan of Thomas Kinkade (Painter of Light) calendars, cards and pictures.

The younger kids on the colony are always busy doing something.

They grow up with the other colony kids as their friends, so they have playmates available all the time.

The boys like to go horseback riding and find it a privilege to be included in a colony event such as rounding up the cows in the fall, branding or riding out in the pasture to check the cows.

Even at a young age, they like to be included in the adult colony members' activities.

Their latest excitement is the new filly that was born earlier this week. Every day after school they go check up on it, to make sure its mommy has enough food, and to try to come up with the perfect name.

The young girls' favorite sport is a game of baseball or catch with their friends. They love jumping on the trampoline, playing Blind Eye Jack, Bush and teaching their pet dog—a collie named Lassie—tricks.

My sister, Gloria, collects baseball cards. The kids also collect "labels for education" for their school.

In the evenings, the girls gather to practice songs for their upcoming spring program. They also like to join the ladies in the garden in the summer and help with vegetable canning.

While school excludes a lot of activities for the kids during the winter months, they take advantage of their summer break, spending as much of their time as possible outdoors enjoying nature.

They are looking forward to their last day of school on May 31.

Little Fish Teach Big Lessons to Colony Kids

Several months ago I bought an aquarium for my little sisters with the money they'd been saving from doing their chores around the house.

Last week, when we added a larger type of goldfish, I made a mental note to myself that I needed to find a new home for some of our smaller fish so our tank wouldn't be overcrowded. I just couldn't think of anyone who would enjoy their company and provide them with a nice, caring home.

This past week I'd been on my sisters' case to go weed our lawn (since most of the grass didn't make it through the winter, weeds were starting to take over). They'd given me a deaf ear all morning. When I went to lunch that day and was helping out in the kids' dining room, I got an idea.

"Do any of you kids want to help me weed our lawn this afternoon?" I asked. None of them even bothered to look up.

"I'm awarding a goldfish to the one with the most weeds when they're finished," I continued.

Suddenly heads turned my way and hands shot into the air. "I'll help!"

"Me, too."

"Count me in."

I smiled approvingly. My sisters didn't! They were offended by my request and they made me well aware of it. I left them with the reminder that I had asked them several times to do the job, and they had refused.

The aquarium had become an attraction for all the colony kids when we first got it. Each time we'd add something new or get a new fish, they'd all come to check things out.

So when I mentioned giving away a fish, I immediately had everyone's attention.

Right after lunch, without having to pass on a hint-filled reminder, I found about ten kids scattered throughout our yard, eager to get a headstart. They worked together in groups, brothers and sisters helping each other out, each hoping that their helpers' contribution would add enough to be the prize winner. My sisters helped too, of course. They picked out their friends whom they hoped would win.

When they finished, they presented their bags to me and silently waited for me to announce the winner. I told them they had all worked extra hard at the project and that each of them had put in equal effort. And though some had pulled more weeds than others, I promised them I'd give each family of kids who helped one goldfish. But they'd have to go home and get permission from their parents first.

They did, and a little while later they each came back with an empty fish jar with a small layer of rocks on the bottom, eager to claim their prize.

I presented them each with a fish. Then, after making them sit through my twenty-minute lecture on the do's and don'ts of caring for fish, they left smiling, proud to show their parents their newest member of the family.

It turned out to be a wonderful afternoon. All the colony kids learned a good lesson: What counted was the good job they did, not who worked the fastest or who could fill their bags with weeds the quickest. My sisters, too, learned a lesson. They now know what happens when not being obedient for their older sister.

As for me, I was content with the thought that I had finally found nice homes for my little friends and that someone was taking good care of them.

You'd Think Cleaning Up after Making Soap Would Be a Breeze, but It's Not

Each spring, Hutterite colonies cook their annual supply of laundry soap. Cooking soap is a conservative way of cleaning up all the old lard and crackling (the residue that's left after rendering lard from fat) that has accumulated over the year.

To start the event, the soap cooked the previous year is ground into powder by a couple of the guys, using a homemade soap grinder. Made from scratch by the men, the apparatus consists of used parts from an old feed grinder.

Two older women are in charge of the soap-making, but each year two different women (and their husbands or brothers) take turns helping.

The soap is cooked in large four-by-eight-by-three-foot vats. The cooking is done outside so that the cool breezes can keep the soap from boiling over and later help it thicken faster in the molds.

A single recipe consists of four hundred pounds of lard and crackling, one hundred pounds of lye, seventy-five gallons of water and eight cups of salt. It normally takes two days to cook seven batches. When it's done, it averages out to about two tons of soap.

The batch takes up to three and a half hours to cook. Then it's set aside to settle for a half hour. As it settles, the soap rises to the top. The lye, which remains at the bottom, is later drained.

Next, the soap is poured into forty-five-inch-by-eight-foot molds. It's allowed to dry and harden for a few hours, before being cut up into small bricks and put into empty onion sacks. The guys hang the sacks in an old Quonset hut where it can stay dry and get plenty of fresh air. The soap is stored there for a whole year to dry and harden until it's time again to make soap. Then it's ground up and ready for use.

The soap is mainly used as laundry detergent. It's very strong and cleans quite well, time and again.

The whole soap-cooking process is one of the biggest, messiest jobs you can imagine. But cleaning up is the worst part. It's a tough job cleaning off the dried soap on the cement floor.

Before we begin, the guys tape wide strips of black tarp on the floor in the cooking area. But with all the walking back and forth, things still get messy.

The job can also be dangerous. The cooks wear heavy protective clothes to avoid direct contact with the lye. Anyone who gets splashed must rinse thoroughly with water.

Soap-cooking has been part of my culture for hundreds of years. The tradition was brought here from Russia, where its name originated—Russian Soap. And until there becomes a better way of cleaning up the old crackling and lard without throwing it away, it's a tradition that will remain.

Kitchen Duties Keep Hutterite Colony Cooking

I've received many letters from people asking me to write about cooking, or just write a piece that includes the ladies in the colony. I guess it's high time that I do.

Most times I take for granted the ladies in the colony, because I'm around them every day. To me, our daily events are not anything new or out of the ordinary. But to the public's eye, they are unique and fascinating.

When people ask what my profession is, I answer homemaker. But many don't realize the home I'm talking about is a small Hutterite community of fifty to sixty people.

Since everyone eats together three times a day at the community kitchen, we spend a fair amount of time preparing food. At the age of seventeen (two years after becoming an adult) a girl gets a "cook week," in which she takes turns cooking with the rest of the ladies. Normally, a woman retires from cooking at the age of fifty.

During that week, the main cook and her helper are excused from all colony activities. Their only responsibility is to cook what's on the schedule for that week.

One rank above the cooks is the "head cook." Her job isn't weekly, but year-round. She's also excused from all colony duties, and her responsibility is permanent, until she feels she can no longer handle it. The job then will be handed down to another lady, elected by the colony's church.

The head cook's job is to prepare all the meats. She makes sure enough food gets prepared every day to feed about sixty people and also takes it out of the freezer to thaw out. Each Friday she fills out the menu for the following week and discusses meal plans with the cooks. The ladies love to try out new recipes—especially desserts and meats.

Sometimes trying new things can be a challenge. Most recipes come in sizes for a single family. First they have to enlarge the recipe, with hopes it'll turn out OK. But most times, when borrowing recipes from other colonies, the chore is already done. In fact, sometimes they're too big, and they have to make them smaller.

It's no secret that homemade pizza comes at the top of the list of favorite foods. Almost everyone where I live is a big pizza fan. Other favorites are spareribs with barbecue sauce (one of my best), pork chops, ham and beans and, of course, steaks and hamburgers.

A regular day in the kitchen starts at 5:30. The hectic seasons are during seeding, spraying and harvest time because of the many lunch buckets there are to make.

Many people wonder if the guys are allowed to cook. The husbands help their wives with odd chores around the kitchen (mostly janitorial duties, such as washing rugs, taking away the garbage, washing the vegetables they need for that week, etc.).

But preparing the meals is out of the question. For one, with the spices they prefer in food, sometimes it is too much, and cleaning up is not particularly in their category. It's not looked at as to who can do it best, but what's best for the colony.

We feel a woman's place is in the kitchen and home while a man's place is in the shop or barn. Besides, with all the activities going on at the shop, maintenance around our farm, etc., they wouldn't have time to cook too.

But each fall at our harvest festival, when we have a roasted pig, a couple of the men get the chore of preparing it in a huge barbecue outside the kitchen. All our smoked food, such as hams, salami, sausage, fish, chicken and turkey, are prepared by the men.

Cooking and trying to please so many people can be a big challenge sometimes.

So it's an old joke that when one of the guys makes a stingy comment about the food, he'll get the answer of, "You want a cook week? Keep it up."

So far, there haven't been any male volunteers, so we must be doing something right.

Colony Shares Whole Wheat Bread, Holiday Bun Recipes

I often receive letters from readers asking me to share colony recipes, especially for our buns and bread. So I've decided to dedicate this column to a few kitchen favorites.

One warning: Our recipes are enlarged to feed a whole colony, not just one family.

WHOLE WHEAT BREAD

4   cups milk
6   cups water
1/4   cup yeast
1/2   cup honey
1/2   cup brown sugar
1   tbsp. salt
1   tsp. arcady powder (preservative available
     at the grocery store—optional)
2   tbsp. molasses
1/3   cup chicken fat
1/3   cup bacon or pork lard
10   cups whole wheat flour
12   cups white flour

Have the dough on the soft side.

Mix honey, salt, sugar, molasses and lards the day before. Set in fridge overnight. Scald milk. Add water and leave in fridge overnight. The next day pour milk/water into mixer. Add enough flour to make a soft paste. Add yeast and arcady powder, mix really well. Add rest of flour and mix for 5-7 minutes. Dough should be tight. Wait 15 minutes and add rest of mixture. Mix for another 5 minutes. Let dough rise for 45 minutes. Cut 20-ounce loaves. Wait 10 minutes before rolling out dough.

Roll together to make a loaf. Let rise on pan 1 to 2 hours. Bake at 300-325 degrees for 18 minutes. (Convection oven. Ovens vary.) This recipe makes 10 loaves, but usually we bake 50 at a time.

HOLIDAY BUN RECIPE

2   cups honey
8   cups lard (half butter and half pork or chicken)
13   cups sugar
3/4   cup salt
11   qt. milk
1 1/2   cups yeast
18   cups water

Mix together honey, lards, sugar and salt the day before and set in fridge. Scald milk, add water and set in room temperature overnight. Put water/milk into mixer and enough white flour to make a paste. Add yeast. Add half of mixture. Mix well for about 5 minutes. Add enough flour to make a medium-tight dough. Add rest of mixture. Let it mix for another 3 minutes or until nice and smooth. Let rise 1 hour. Knead down by hand. Let rise another hour. Cut and roll buns. Let buns rise 1½ to 2 hours on pans. Bake at 300 degrees in convection oven 12-15 minutes. (Note: we do not have a measurement for our flour.)

This bun recipe is what we use at weddings, funerals and holidays. It is a little sweeter than our regular bun recipe, but very good.

Hutterite colonies are constantly swapping recipes, especially for desserts. The ladies also subscribe to many cookbooks.

If any readers decide to try these recipes, I would love to hear the results.

Colony Women Work Hard in Living Quarters, for Benefit of All

Though each Hutterite colony's building designs are unique, with variations in size and shape, the general building style never changes; it just improves as the years go by.

A colony's living quarters are always set away from the barns and garage. The ladies of the colony manage the living quarters and don't generally work in the barns and fields. The areas are not restricted, and the women and girls certainly are free to visit, but it is mostly the domain of the guys. I'll write about those areas next week.

The church is designed to seat all the colony members, as well as have extra room left for a large wedding or funeral. In most cases, the church will be attached to the communal kitchen, but there are some cases (in older, established colonies) where the church stands alone.

The communal kitchen is the largest building in a colony's living quarters. It has the most activities happening year-round.

Since all the colony members meet at the kitchen daily for meal-

Women on kitchen duty at Gildford Colony bake "schneki," a moderately sweet German cookie.

time, it is set up to cook for, and then seat and feed, a large group of people at one time.

There is a large dining room where the adults eat. Like at church, the men sit on one side and the women sit on the other—all according to age.

The cooking area is spacious with large equipment (similar to that of a restaurant) including a broasting pan, oven, deep fryer and large steam kettles for soup.

There is no dishwasher—the ladies are divided into two groups, and they take turns washing dishes weekly. Every colony has a large walk-in cooler and freezer.

The children's dining room is separate from the adults'. The children are under close supervision by the German schoolteacher and his wife. From age five to their fifteenth birthday, the children eat in the children's dining room. They are responsible for cleaning the room, washing their own dishes and setting the tables.

The ladies take weekly turns in the colony's bakery. There is a dough mixer large enough to handle the colony's weekly supply of bread or buns at one time. The bakery also is equipped with two ovens, for the convenience of the baker.

Attached to the kitchen is also the laundry room, where you'll find four to six washing machines and two dryers.

Each family is responsible for their own laundry. The colony provides the laundry soap, which is made each spring and ground into powder after it has hardened for a year.

Sometimes even the colony's slaughterhouse is attached to the kitchen; sometimes it isn't. There all the butchering is done, including cutting and packing the meat and making sausage. In the summertime, the ladies spend most of their time in the slaughterhouse canning the colony's winter supply of vegetables. The slaughterhouse is equipped with large kettles for the canning jars.

Every colony has its own English school building, in which the lessons are taught in English. (Other lessons in German are taught in the church building.) It also is part of the living quarters and is equipped with a playground for the children, which usually includes a baseball field, swings, a slide, monkey bars, etc.

The colony homes usually are connected in a line of four to six units, to save space. Each family has its own apartment. When a couple gets married, a furnished home is provided for them as a wedding gift from the colony.

The living quarters are constantly engaged with activities by the women and children, but usually keeping up the repairs and yard work is a shared responsibility by both genders of all ages.

In my next column, I'll tell about the barns, garage and other areas where the men engage in their work.

Men Cover Many Different Jobs in Barns and Garage

In my last column, I covered the colony's living quarters, specifically the ladies' area of work. Today I'll explain the barns and garage, the domain of the guys.

The first structures to be built at a new colony are the barns. This is so there will be a steady income to support the new colony.

Most Hutterite colonies raise beef cattle and hogs. There will be a large pig operation of usually two hundred pigs or more. One specific guy is in charge of the pig barns. He will have a helper, as well as several younger guys under his training and supervision.

The ranch cow boss also has a helper and several guys working to learn the trade. The ranch cow boss will have several hundred head of cattle in his care, along with a handful of working ranch horses. There is a special area among the colony's corrals set aside for the calving season, by far the busiest time of year for the cowboys.

A colony's milk barn can range from five milking cows, only for colony use, to up to two hundred when the milk is sold commercially.

Ranch cows and milk cows aren't taken care of by the same guy, as it would be too much. The milkman is assisted by his wife, who is excused from all other colony work during milking hours. Until she retires, she is permanently excused from activities such as cooking and baking.

Hutterite colonies all raise ducks, geese, chickens and turkeys for their own use, as a year-round meat source. Again, a specific guy is in charge of the poultry.

Many colonies also raise sheep. Although several guys are in charge of caring for the sheep, shearing time is a joint effort and everyone helps.

The colony's garage is a busy place, very much like the kitchen. There is always a tractor to repair or a flat tire to fix. The garage has two departments—one section where the repairs are done, the other for blacksmithing. A guy is in charge of each of those jobs.

The carpentry shop usually is booming with activities as well. During the summer months, repairs and major building jobs are normally done around the colony. During the winter months, indoor work, such as making furniture, is done. That job normally keeps two to three guys busy.

The colony's electrical work is handled by one guy, as is the plumbing. They each have their separate rooms to store their tools and supplies. Whenever something is broken and needs to be fixed, there are usually enough supplies in stock to make the repair.

The colony also has its own generator; should a major outage happen, the colony is never more than a few minutes without power. This way, the fans and water in the barns don't stop, and things like milking and mealtime aren't delayed.

Many colonies also are engaged in small "wintertime" jobs, such as bookbinding, shoemaking, shoe repair and broom-making.

Colony land is taken care of by the field boss. He gives the special instructions of seeding, combining, etc.

When a new colony is started, there are experienced contractors who work with the colony's carpenter to draw the blueprints. Many of these contractors work specifically in colony design and layout.

Biblical Tradition, Day-to-Day Events Determine Men's Clothes

All the men's clothes are home-sewn. Each family does its own sewing, occasionally with the help of friends and relatives from other colonies.

The men only are allowed to wear black pants. They must wear suspenders at all times, and it would be considered inappropriate to walk around without their shirts tucked in.

Although unnoticeable to the general public, the men do have different clothes for different occasions.

Dress pants and work pants are made of different types of material.

Work shirts are darker than dress shirts worn to church, which are white with occasional vertical-line patterns.

When the guys go to church, they wear a long black jacket with long sleeves made of special suiting material; it's known in German as a "yanker." The men also wear their church jackets for other important occasions, such as a church council meeting, Sunday breakfast, weddings, etc. Boys are required to wear their church jackets when attending German school and Sunday school.

Men and women wear church jackets to church and the evening prayer meetings to show respect.

The patterns the men in the three groups of Hutterites wear are much the same. The general dress code is multi-colored shirts, suspenders and black pants. Dariusleut and Schmiedeleut men are allowed to wear snaps in their shirts; Lehrerleut men can only wear buttons. Unlike the Dariusleut and Lehrerleut, the Schmiedeleut can wear short-sleeved shirts.

The men always wear caps or hats to work and around the colony. The only exception is when they are attending church, at home or eating at the communal dining room. Corinthians 11:4 reads, "Every man who prays or prophesies with his head covered dishonors his head." That is why you will never see a Hutterite man eating with his hat or cap on.

Boys' clothes are no different than their fathers', other than when they are little, they tend to wear caps instead of hats.

The ladies choose the material for the men's clothes. The bolts are ordered from the same companies where the ladies get their dress material. Usually two patterns are picked at one time; each man will get two shirts.

Apparel Women, Girls Wear
Depends on Occasion, Sect

When it comes to teen girls' clothes, especially dresses, it seems one can never have enough.

But the colony gives each female several dresses a year. (Hutterite women also can buy dresses for themselves from stores.) They get to choose from a variety of colors and samples sent to the colonies each spring by several large fabric manufacturers. In at least one case, the manufacturer specializes in material it knows will be appropriate and acceptable for the colony ladies to wear. Those samples are especially designed for Hutterites, since we account for about ninety-five percent of their business.

Much of the material is ordered by the bolt. Cotton, interlock and Softique are popular types. In the past few years, rayon, crepe and peachskin have become popular as well.

Although the patterns of all of our dresses are the same, we have different types of dresses for different occasions. We also use certain types of material only for certain dresses. Cotton is generally used for everyday wear, cooking and working in the garden. Interlock and softique, when new, are worn for Saturday and Sunday. In time, they will be passed on as an everyday dress. Rayon, crepe and peachskin are only worn for weekend clothes and on special occasions such as holidays and weddings.

A wedding dress for a bride is different. This is made out of special material, usually satin, and is royal blue.

When a girl gets baptized, she wears a black satin or rayon dress when attending the seven weeks of classes before being baptized. We also wear black dresses at Easter, out of respect for Jesus' death, and when attending funerals. Surprising as this might seem, I've noticed that black dresses (with multi-colored flowers and designs on them) are also being worn for weekend dresses the last year or so.

We also wear black church jackets (with long sleeves) when attending church and evening prayer meetings. Young girls are required to wear their church jackets when attending Sunday and German school.

There are three groups of Hutterites, the Lehrerleut, the Schmiedeleut and the Dariusleut, to which I belong.

The Dariusleut ladies' dress is a three-piece outfit, and the vest, skirt and apron are all made of the same material. Girls ages one to nine wear two-piece dresses. When they feel comfortable and are of age, they get to wear the three-piece dress.

The Dariusleut ladies also wear scarves with small polka-dots on them. The Bible, First Corinthians; Chapter 11; verses 5 and 10, says women should cover their heads. I'm told the polka-dots have no significance, that's just the way it's always been.

Little girls wear a bonnet, known in German as a "mitz." They usually wear the bonnet until age five or six, around the time they start attending German and English school. The adult ladies do their hair in the front in a "twist," which is then secured in a bun in the back. Little girls' hair is braided until they are capable of doing their hair without assistance from their mom or older siblings.

The Lehrerleut are generally considered more conservative. The ladies wear a four-piece outfit—a vest, skirt, apron and jacket to match their dress. The vest, skirt, and jacket are made of the same material, but the apron is different. They do their hair in a twist like the Dariusleut, but they wear scarves with large polka-dots instead of small ones like the Dariusleut.

The little girls wear a dress outfit similar to their mothers' and also wear their hair in a twist. They, too, wear a mitz until they start school.

The Schmiedeleut dress style is much different from the Dariusleut and Lehrerleut. Their ladies wear a two-piece outfit—only a vest and skirt, made of the same material. They don't twist their hair, but comb it back and secure it in a bun. The girls have the same dress and hairstyle, but also wear a mitz until ready to start school. Then they wear a scarf with small, almost unnoticeable polka-dots like the adult ladies.

Most Schmiedeleut colonies are in Canada, the Dakotas and Minnesota.

Colony Seamstresses
Add Improvements to Old Styles

At a single glance, what makes Hutterites stand out in a crowd is their clothes.

They're not worn to attract attention or to introduce a new trend, even though they draw many curious glances their way. It's the Hutterite way of separating themselves from "die Welt," a popular Hutterite phrase meaning, "the world."

The clothes we wear originated in the 1700s, and the styles were brought with us on our journey from Russia to America in 1874.

The styles may seem unchanged to outsiders for perhaps a century, but that's hardly the situation.

Though the styles themselves don't change too dramatically, Hutterite seamstresses find many ways to improve them. The older ladies find that "sewing was much simpler 'back then.'" The complicated methods the younger generation is taking to improve the Hutterite garb—especially men's church jackets—are overwhelming, they say.

On the other hand, up-to-date Hutterite seamstresses are eager to try a new challenge. They personally enjoy working at redesigning patterns in hopes of finding the perfect fit.

When a girl is baptized in a Dariusleut colony, she gets a sewing machine of her choice as a baptismal gift from the colony. Until that time comes, young girls get sewing lessons from their mothers, older sisters or aunts, so by the time they get their own sewing machines they are trained and sewing on their own. The most popular sewing machines are Pfaff and Bernina.

Every colony has several older ladies elected for the job of being the "material cutters." They are in charge of ordering, cutting and equally dividing the material the colony gets for each member.

There are several occasions when a Hutterite boy or girl gets special "extra" clothes. When a baby is born, the family receives a package of material as a baby gift from the colony. At the age of three, when boys and girls enter the German class of kindergarten school, they're given extra dresses, shirts and pants as play clothes.

Lisa's sisters, Lorraine, Rhoda, and Gloria, hang the family wash on a homemade clothesline.

When young Hutterites approach adulthood at age fifteen, they get a large assortment of material for dresses, shirts and other apparel. They also receive accessories, such as a butcher knife and butcher's apron.

Choosing material is lots of fun, especially when it comes to choosing a new dress. Every spring, large material manufacturers, such as Mook, Marshall and Mitchell, send their latest samples of dresses, men's shirts, etc., to all the colonies. Then the ladies gather at the communal kitchen to do the choosing.

Several weeks later, when the material arrives at the colony, it is cut and equally divided among all the members and genders.

When It Comes to New Fashion Trends, Hutterite Teens Feel Peer Pressure, Too

I opened my bedroom closet in search of a Sunday dress to wear for the prayer meeting Saturday evening. Letting out a sigh, I glanced over the half dozen or more rayon dresses, trying to make a good choice.

What should I wear? The solid gray or aqua, or the blue with flowers, the one I just finished several days back. Or maybe the dark-tan Peachskin—a buddy dress—which several of my close friends and I got at the same time.

I sew all my own clothes—and my family's. Since very little of our clothing is purchased, I get a lot of practice. But it's something I enjoy very much and spend a lot of time doing, since I come from a family of nine.

My mother interrupts my thoughts. "Lisa, are you getting ready for gebete (prayer meeting)? You only have a half hour," she called down to the basement.

"Yes," I answered. "I just need to get dressed and do my hair. I'll be right up."

I made a quick choice, grabbed the dress my brother had given me as a Christmas gift last year and hurried into the bathroom to do my hair. Several minutes later, my brother knocked on the door. "Another hour?" he asked. I ignored his sarcastic comment and finished doing my hair.

My thoughts began to wander as I put on my dress.

I recalled the time when I borrowed my best friend's first rayon dress. All my friends already had several before I got my first one. My friend's dress drew the attention of the older ladies right away.

"Lisa, where did you get that dress from? Why, I still recall when my mother had a dress that looked almost exactly like yours."

I was both surprised and amazed. But mostly I was stunned to be wearing a new-style dress that was popular more than half a century ago.

I got the same reaction when high-top girls' shoes came out. To any teen, it seemed, the taller the heel, the bulkier the look and better to wear.

When the smaller eyeglass frames became popular, I was sure history was repeating itself in styles.

Hutterite youths seem to take to the styles right away. So, of course, if you see your friends wearing something new—you have to get it too, so you don't feel out of place.

Many people don't realize how much peer pressure there is among the Hutterite teens—especially with clothes. When I asked my mom what she wore to fit in with the crowd as a teen, she answered with a sigh, "When I grew up, we didn't have peer pressure. Not at school, not at home—certainly not like you girls do today. I guess you could say we weren't as adventurous to try out different things. I didn't have to worry about trying to compete with my friends with new clothes. We were more conservative back then."

I closed my eyes and tried to imagine myself as my mom about four decades ago. I couldn't.

Peer pressure is definitely the toughest part of growing up in the twenty-first century for any teen, no matter what culture they're from. I know, because I personally can relate.

Hutterite Teen Likes
Insider Glimpse of Life at GFH

Several weeks back, a reporter from the Great Falls High School paper called to get my permission for an interview.

The first thing that impressed me was being interviewed by a student reporter—someone my own age. (I don't come in contact with a lot of teens interested in journalism.) The second was having the interview, along with an article I was asked to write, published in their school paper.

The thought brought back floods of memories of the time I was the publisher of our school paper. When I graduated, the paper was the hardest to let go. I had started it from scratch and didn't have enough time to train the younger students to take over by the time the end of the school year came around.

So there I was, lost in a past memory over a single phone call.

A week after the interview, I received a newsletter in the mail from the Great Falls High School Iniwa. I was pleased with the whole page—the color, the graphics design, the layout, the questions and answers of my interview—everything.

I asked Ian Gray, the senior who interviewed me, if I could tour the paper, since I was going to Great Falls the following week. He gladly agreed, so we set up a meeting.

I guess the "tour of the school paper" is a story by itself. After being introduced to the staff of reporters, photographers and editor, they explained how their system works. Then they asked if I'd like a tour of the school. "It'll only take fifteen minutes."

"Sure," I said. I had some time, and it isn't every day I get such an offer.

The tour started with three students from the paper staff and the student president. I'm guessing my tour guides were as interested in me as I was in them. They had zillions of questions, but so did I. They weren't at all embarrassed to stroll around their campus with a Hutterite girl their age, exchanging information from two totally different cultures. In fact, they seemed to enjoy the experience, because as the tour went on, more students joined.

I was introduced to everybody—or so it seemed. Students, teachers—I even met an exchange student from Germany. And yes, she understood my German dialogue, even though she thought she wouldn't.

As we went from classroom to classroom, I took notice of something that inspired me about this group. For meeting me for the first

Women and children from the Surprise Creek Colony return home after taking the menfolk coffee and snacks.

time, they seemed to know which classes I'd be acquainted with and most knowledgeable of. For example, they asked if I'd like to tour the cooking class, sewing and the carpentry shop—classes I'm familiar with at the colony, though they are taught out of school.

My mind began to wander. What would I have done if I had such opportunities when I attended high school?

Attending grades nine to twelve at the colony school through correspondence courses was a privilege for young eighth-grade graduates. It was the best and only way to get a higher education than eighth grade without going to a school in town—something the elders in the colonies didn't approve of. Yes, what would I have done?

Not only had I come in contact with a great school, but also some awesome students. Their thoughtfulness impressed me immensely, as well as their well-mannered, caring and mature attitudes. I felt no hint of prejudice.

Walking to our car over an hour later left me floating a few inches off the ground. What a great afternoon, I thought. I'd never been around so many teenagers at once—in my life!

I wondered what they would have said had I told them I was the only one in my grade in our small country school at the colony.

Then I remembered something. I did have something they didn't— I never had to fight hall rush-hour madness.

Trips to Town a Treat, Especially for Ladies

Everyone on the colony looks forward to a trip to town or visit to another colony.

When someone goes to town, it usually means that person has a doctor's appointment. For the men, sometimes, it's different. It's a part of their everyday work. They get to go away more often than the ladies for other reasons, like getting parts for a tractor, attending a farm or ranch meeting or hauling wheat to the elevator in town.

For the ladies, trips to town are a bit of fun mixed with pleasure, such as packing lunch for a picnic at the park and going shopping in between appointments.

My colony's closest town for doctor's appointments is Havre. For medical treatment unavailable in Havre, we usually go to Great Falls.

At 130 miles one way, going to Great Falls is an all-day affair. We get up and have an early breakfast and leave no later than six o'clock in the morning.

Going shopping is lots of fun, something all the ladies love to do. We tend to shop mostly in the big discount stores such as Wal-Mart, Kmart, ShopKo and Target. When taking inventory for the colony's groceries, we shop at big wholesale stores like Sam's Club and Ryan's Cash and Carry.

A favorite "must do" on trips to town is stopping at the library for a stack of books and picking up a cappuccino or ice cream for the drive home.

Trips to other colonies are fairly frequent. The ladies go home to visit their families for a two-week trip during the winter months. If there is a ride going in that direction during the spring, summer and fall months, if it suits their schedule, the ladies will join the trip to visit their relatives for a weekend.

An old favorite tradition in my colony is taking a Sunday afternoon cruise to a neighboring Lehrerleut colony and spending the day with them. It is also vice versa for them. The trips are most times unannounced, to be a "surprise visit." These trips are usually reserved for the ladies and are special because we all get to travel together and spend the afternoon with friends.

During the summer months, if we are lacking a certain vegetable in the garden, the ladies will make reservations to go to another colony for these vegetables. There we will join the ladies from that colony in helping pick the vegetables and prepare them for the drive home.

Usually in July, on a nice calm day, the ladies will snag one of the men to take us Juneberry picking. We'll pack sandwiches, chips and pop for a picnic lunch. Then for supper we'll take along hamburgers and hot dogs to barbecue. As the day comes to an end, our driver will start up a fire and will call for us when he's ready to start barbecuing the hamburgers.

Then we'll all sit down to a welcoming supper after a tiring but enjoyable outing.

Reading is a Favorite Pastime on the Colony

If you asked my sister Gloria what life is about (in a nutshell), she'd answer: "Reading a book. And no chores—ever!"

She, along with her other sisters, just discovered their love for reading, so most of the time they're lost in Reading Wonderland. In fact, reading happens to be the most popular pastime for Hutterites.

Some of our favorite authors are Laura Ingalls Wilder and Christian writers Janette Oke and Karen Kingsbury, who also happen to be favorites among most of the other colony ladies.

Reading materials vary greatly in a colony. It all depends on the person's interest. Some of the ladies subscribe to *Quick Cooking, Taste of Home, Country Woman, Women's World, Guideposts* and *Readers' Digest*. They make frequent visits to our local library for reading materials.

My current interest is looking for books written by Hutterite authors about Hutterite life or the Hutterite culture. Each search leaves me surprised at the amount of Hutterite literature available to the public. I find most of these books amusing because of their authors' imaginations. Since many weren't born and raised in the Hutterite culture, much of the information is questionable, and sometimes libelous.

Some reading material is frowned upon in our culture, such as trashy magazines or tabloids. What one reads is not reviewed by the elders but is left to each individual's judgment and common sense. The books our children read are viewed and approved by their parents to make sure they are suitable.

The colony usually subscribes to a main statewide newspaper (the *Great Falls Tribune*, in our case) which is passed around and shared. Reading the newspaper is something the older colony members look forward to and enjoy doing the most.

We also have lots of German literature available to read. All our church sermons are printed in High German, as are our song books. We also have the New Testament in German, which we read out of in our homes and during our Sunday school classes. There are many more German books found in our homes, such as *Confession of Faith* by Peter Reideman, the Holy Bible and Hutterite history books, to name a few.

Our men tend to find their reading interest lies in areas related to their colony occupation.

My brother Brian has an overactive interest in modern seeding equipment, tractors, trucks and pickups. He serves as a wonderful research resource when I write about the men doing the seeding and combining during the spring and summer months. A big lover of Ford, John Deere and Peterbilt, he has a large selection of their latest brochures. He's a subscriber to most farm magazines available in his field—*Farm Industry News, Light and Medium Truck, Overdrive, Owner Operator* and more.

Brian has a special passion for John Deere tractors. Our oldest brother, Ernie, says he has the "Green Paint Disease."

Every winter, after attending the annual MAGIE in Great Falls and the Ag Expo in Lethbridge, he floats a few inches off the ground. It takes him about a week or so before his head pops out of the stacks of brochures he collected at the farm shows.

His present interest is checking out Global Positioning Systems, since we started seeding and spraying with the use of a GPS device last spring.

Ernie, the cowboy in our family, loves to read ranch, cow and horse magazines such as *Drover, Western Horseman, Beef Today* and a ranching newspaper called *Agri News – the Best in the West.* He's also a big fan of Louis L'Amour books.

Each year when I do our annual spring cleaning, I go through my brothers' stacks and stacks of magazines, brochures and books. I sort in my "to throw away" pile everything except the last two months' issues. Of course, I have two not-so-happy brothers after they find out about it.

They keep a watchful eye on me to make sure I don't destroy any important "guy treasures."

Spring Cleaning Less of a Chore with a Little Help from Friends

Spring is here—my favorite season. And so is spring cleaning.

As the season drew near, the ladies at my colony were faced with a tough decision. How were we going to get all the colony buildings cleaned with the few women available this year?

With the womanpower already low at our colony, we knew we'd be shorthanded this year. Two of the ladies were excused from all colony duties because of maternity leave, while several others had gone to help out at a colony emergency. This left us with only five ladies to do the cleaning.

So the older ladies had a meeting to decide how our cleaning schedule was going to work out. The conclusion they came to was to ask our Lehrerleut neighbors to help us out.

Montana has two types of Hutterite colonies, the Dariusleut, which my colony belongs to, and the more conservative Lehrerleut.

A single phone call to the Sage Creek Hutterian Colony, twenty miles north of Chester, brought us the answer we were hoping for. Fifteen ladies immediately volunteered to come help out.

Arrangements were made to pick up and deliver the cleaners that same day. Arriving just before breakfast in our two vans, we shared a hearty breakfast with our friends. Shortly after that, we began cleaning our kitchen.

Everywhere you looked, you saw a group of ladies doing something different. One group started washing all the dishes, while another began cleaning the cupboards. Another party was working on the tile ceiling, while another began cleaning the walls.

It was a project that normally took our ladies two weeks. But with the extra help, we cleaned both the up and downstairs in one day—something none of our ladies thought possible.

Dinner was at 11:30. The cooks prepared a luncheon of beef stew and the extras. It was our first real break that morning to sit, relax, and exchange news between the two colonies.

The afternoon seemed to float by like a breeze and things seemed to go much faster. The last room was finished just as the supper bell rang. Then we sat down to a delicious meal of fried chicken and the trimmings—a favorite of our Lehrerleut friends.

Our ladies were impressed by the willing help we received that day, but even more by the wonderful job that was done. There wasn't a tile that didn't shine or a window that didn't sparkle.

When we took the cleaners home that evening (an hour's drive from our colony), we couldn't thank them enough for the favor they had done for us. And before we left for home that night, our friends once again volunteered to come the next week to help us with the rest of the buildings.

It was an offer we couldn't turn down, so the following week we made arrangements for a different crew to come. We finished the rest of the colony buildings by two that afternoon and spent the rest of the day visiting and going for walks around the colony showing them our farm.

The simple words "thank you" don't seem to express enough our gratitude and appreciation for such a big favor. Our friends did for us in two days what would have taken our ladies a whole month.

In our society, this act of goodness is called "Helping out the Christian Church." It's an art, we learned, that hasn't been forgotten. And with friends like the Sage Creek Colony, we have a perfect example.

Best Friend is Treasure for Lifetime

My best friend, Leona, celebrated her fifteenth birthday last week.

Like all Hutterite boys and girls, she couldn't wait for the big day when she would finally be recognized as an adult.

Turning fifteen cuts a lot of boundaries in Hutterite life. I guess the biggest and most looked-forward-to is no longer eating in the kids' dining room.

The second is graduating from "German school" where we learn our language and study our religion. German classes are held before and after regular school classes each day.

And there's one more thing to look forward to. When a boy or girl becomes an adult, he or she is presented with several expensive gifts from the colony.

The biggest is a dresser made by the colony's carpenter. He has three or four styles to choose from.

Several days before Leona's fifteenth birthday, she came from Saskatchewan to pay us a visit. We planned a surprise party for her one evening during her stay. The party was a complete surprise, but beyond that, I think she was more surprised by my choice of a birthday gift—a custom-made Hutterite rolling pin.

Just before I varnished it, I asked her mother to engrave her full name and the date of her fifteenth birthday on it.

You might wonder why I chose this specific item as a gift. When I turned fifteen, I received a rolling pin as a gift from my colony. Such a gift is known as a "girlhood treasure"—something that isn't used anymore, but is simply hung up for decoration. Since my friend's colony doesn't have a carpentry shop as advanced as ours, she probably wouldn't get a rolling pin from anyone else, and I knew how much my gift would mean to her.

Our friendship formed when we were young kids. She would come to visit my grandparents several times during the year and would spend several weeks at my colony in the summer. Now that she's fifteen, she has to work with the rest of the adult women workforce at home, and we won't be able to see each other as much and spend the summers together. Last year, as her summer visit came to an end, she said to me one evening, "This is going to be our last summer together, but out of all of them, this one was the very best."

We're both interested in the same stuff. For example, we'd probably skip a shopping trip to town and go horseback riding instead. We both love adventure!

Clothes are the big deal for us. Both our mothers are still trying to figure out when we'll outgrow the love of wearing each other's clothes—especially dresses and shoes. I've yet to figure out why we love each other's fashion tastes more than our own.

But that's not the most important part of our friendship. What we both treasure the most is being able to spend time together to just talk, share secrets, smiles as well as tears and catch up on each others' lives.

We try not to forget important holidays such as birthdays, Christmas and Easter. If something happens, we'll call or write to tell each other the news.

I think the best years of our friendship are right now, while we're still young and single. In the next decade, when we're in our twenties and perhaps marry, we won't get to spend as much time with each other. But we'll still find excuses to visit and help each other out.

And somewhere along the line, occasionally we'll find something to argue or disagree about. We might tell each other something the other one doesn't want to hear. But that's what a true and honest friendship is all about.

When all is said and done, there isn't anything in this material world we'd trade or find more valuable than our friendship, because we see it as a precious token of love.

Teen Proud of Historic Collection at High Plains Heritage Center

Recently, I was invited to tour the High Plains Heritage Center in Great Falls to see a newly donated collection of Hutterite artifacts.

Unfamiliar with the valuable collection, one of the ladies at the museum wanted someone to come and explain what everything was so they could put up proper identification cards.

I asked my grandparents to join me for the tour because I knew their wisdom and knowledge would come in handy.

They were instantly absorbed in the collection and were able to explain in detail what each item was, along with its significance at the time it was made and what it means to a Hutterite today.

A highlight for me was the collection of "samplers"—pieces of cloth featuring different styles of cross-stitched letters, numbers, symbols, flower designs and such. They date from the early 1900s through the 1930s.

At the turn of the century young girls would use the samplers to pick out letter styles they would then embroider on handkerchiefs for their beloved. A typical message was, "May God keep you safe for me."

On each piece of cloth you'd find the girl's maiden name, the date when it was made and sometimes the girl's birthday as well. Today it's rare to find such cross-stitched samplers and handkerchiefs among a teenage girl's most valued possessions.

What I found most impressive was a large buggy shawl. It, too, had a girl's maiden name cross-stitched on the back. The shawls were once used like a blanket to keep warm on a cold buggy ride. The shawl instantly caught my interest because I had always wanted to see one. A buggy shawl was a gift from the colony that every girl received when she turned fifteen.

The reason I've never seen one is because they aren't popular in my generation.

When I turned fifteen, I was given the choice of receiving a buggy shawl or a mink blanket. I chose the mink blanket.

Also among the museum's collection was a noodle maker, clothing, several rocking chairs, a hope chest, hand-woven knitting and laundry baskets and some German literature. Each item held strong significance for me because, although they aren't from my generation, they are still part of my heritage.

Though I didn't have enough time to tour the rest of the museum, I'd like to encourage everyone to visit the High Plains Heritage Center, the new home of the Cascade County Historical Society. I'd especially encourage older Hutterites to go see part of their heritage on public display. I know it will make each of you proud to see a part of your past suddenly come to life.

Hutterites Mustn't Let True German Slip Away from Them

I think the most unique thing people find about the Hutterites is the language we speak.

When someone asks me how many languages I speak, I answer, "three"—High German, Low German and English. Some people think Low German and High German are one language, but they aren't.

Our first language is Low German. We speak this fluently in our homes from the time we first learn to talk. In my group, the Dariusleut, more so than the other two groups of Hutterites, a lot of the English language is mixed in with the Low German. In fact, there is so much English mixed in, some Hutterites choose to speak English over German.

Personally, I prefer to speak English and consider it my first language, even though German was taught to me first.

Though in some cases this might seem like a good thing, it isn't always.

It's good in one way: If there is a lot of English spoken in our homes, the younger children pick it up faster, and they speak fluent English by the time they start school.

But because German isn't spoken as much, it's starting to be overlooked. The upcoming generations who don't speak it also don't understand it.

This is a problem, because all our German text is written in High German. It also makes it a tougher job for the German schoolteacher. In German school, we read and write only in High German. There are no texts written in Low German.

There is a reasonable explanation for our tri-lingual status.

Before the Hutterites immigrated to North America, they lived in Russia. When the people communicated amongst themselves, they spoke a form of German infused with Russian.

But in Russia the Hutterites were persecuted for their beliefs. In the 1870s they fled to North America where English was thrown into the mix.

The language has gradually evolved into the Low German we speak today.

According to my grandma, the High German we speak is the true German language. We normally don't have a problem understanding and speaking High German with non-Hutterites who know the language. In fact, I was once told that my grandma had a very High German vocabulary and her communication skills with someone from the "old country" were excellent.

High German is so important in our culture, it's scary to think it's slowly fading away.

Our church sermons and songs will always be written in High German—that will never change. That's why it's so important to keep it studied, understood and taught in our German school so that ten or twenty years from now it's still actively used in our communities, but more importantly, among our young people.

Hutterite Woman Leaves Legacy of Strength, Love to Family

In November 28, my great grandmother, Susie Tschetter (from my father's side) passed away peacefully in her sleep at home in Leader, Saskatchewan. She was eighty-six.

I didn't know her well because, over the past eleven years, she suffered a series of strokes, so her visits to my colony weren't frequent.

Yet my parents and others close to her talk about her often, including about how she inspired their lives. Best of all, she is remembered for her quiet, kind-hearted nature.

As is our tradition, following the death of a colony member, we have a wake the first two evenings before the funeral. At the wakes, all the family, relatives and friends who come to show their last respects gather to sing spiritual songs that relate to death. Occasionally, one of the ministers will give a short speech telling of the wonderful things this person did in her lifetime and the example she left behind for others to follow.

The day of my great grandmother's funeral was peaceful. It started snowing early that morning. As I watched the snow fall softly, it reminded me of Grandma's life. The funeral started shortly after lunch. The sermon was about departing from earth and how short life is. Following the sermon, the pallbearers (eight grandsons and grandsons-in-law) carried the coffin to the nearby graveyard where the body was lowered into the freshly dug grave and buried by the pallbearers.

A true Christian woman, Grandma Susie lived by the words she spoke. The most difficult scenes in her life brought her closer to God. She had been married to Fred Tschetter for six short years when he was killed in a farm accident. Two angry bulls knocked him off his horse while he was out riding one afternoon.

Grandma Susie was left to care for four young children ages five years to three weeks. She never remarried. At first it was hard for her, losing her husband when she was only twenty-eight years old and caring for her family alone, but she turned to God for comfort, strength and encouragement.

Shortly after her husband's death, Grandma Susie was appointed kindergarten schoolteacher at her colony. She taught for thirty-eight years. During this time she also wrote by hand 254 German Hutterite church sermons for a number of ministers.

Grandma Susie suffered her first stroke in 1988. Shortly after that she was in the constant care of her two daughters, her family and many friends. Her younger daughter, Susan, remained single to stay at home to care for her mother, while other family members came for several weeks at a time to help out.

Grandma Susie had been a widow for fifty-eight years when she died. She was never heard complaining of the silent pain she suffered, nor became angry with God. She never accepted anything from anyone without expressing her gratitude and appreciation. Even a hug from a friend she rewarded with a "thank you" and a smile.

The life she led became a symbol for many, especially her twenty-five grandchildren and forty-two great grandchildren who were always surrounding her, listening to the Bible stories she had to tell, the German songs she sang and the love she passed on to others.

Aging Colony Members are Venerated, Cared For

On January 29, my grandparents celebrated their sixty-seventh wedding anniversary.

Both eighty-eight years old, they've lived a life of toil and labor, and together raised a family of fifteen children. Three died in infancy, and they lost their youngest son in an accident at the colony in 1983. They both know the hardships life has for us, but also the joys and blessings.

Both were born in South Dakota. They lived a portion of their lives in Canada, before moving to Montana, where they've lived the past fifty-three years.

They grew up without the advantages of modern technology. Horse and buggy was common transportation early on, but as time went by, they gradually switched to automobiles.

Many new technologies followed, but their generation never let change infringe on the Hutterites' communal lifestyle.

As an ordained minister, it is, in fact, my grandfather's job to lead and teach his colony spiritually, as well as pass on our traditions. He has carried out this responsibility with perfection and merit since 1948.

But during the past decade, as he aged, his responsibilities lessened. Eventually they were passed on to the next generation.

Yet my grandfather's opinion and voice still carry weight in my colony.

The elderly people in a colony have an important role in our society. They are highly respected. It's their responsibility to pass on our way of life. They're the ones to turn to if a major crisis occurs.

For example, if we lost power for an extended period of time or had a water or food emergency, we'd rely on their knowledge and wisdom to get us through.

Their ideas would be of great value to the community, because the world they were brought up in was a lot different than ours, and they are familiar with the ways of living without modern conveniences.

But best yet, the elderly are like a reference library into the past.

So many times when I've needed help with a writing project that involved history, I've turned to my grandparents.

They were there; they lived it, and they knew firsthand the facts of how things happened back then and why. Asking them is like bringing back a recollection or memory of the past.

In our colony, retirement is a personal choice made when one feels they can no longer physically or mentally do their appointed job.

Once an elderly person is retired, they receive the best of care. Of course, they still check up on colony activities and help out when they feel they're able.

None of our elderly folks are put in a nursing home. Their needs are provided for at their colony, in the comfort of their own home, usually by their sons and daughters.

The kids are on call day and night.

If a person doesn't have children, their nieces and nephews take over the task.

As I glimpse the future, I am aware that my own parents will grow old someday. And when the time comes, my siblings and

I will be there to watch over them and tend to their needs.

The responsibility is not looked at as a burden, but as an opportunity to return the love and affection my parents showed when they raised us. It'll be our turn to show we care.

Funeral for Beloved Hutterite Woman Draws Hundreds from Canada, Montana

Golden-ripened wheat fields swayed gently in the afternoon breeze as a large caravan of roughly thirty-five Suburbans, vans and pickups rolled down a remote gravel road.

A colony located along the highway where the party would pass had been on the lookout all afternoon. They all stood waiting in the colony's yard, smiling, waving and counting the cars as they passed.

Other farmers working in the fields stopped what they were doing to look. As the caravan passed through small communities, townsfolk paused for a moment, wondering what the occasion was.

It was unusual for such a large caravan of Hutterites to travel together. Certainly, it was too large for a wedding party.

We were traveling to the Mayfield Colony near Etzikom, Alberta, to bury Susie Stahl.

Stahl, age ninety-six, passed away August 13, at the hospital in Taber, Alberta, surrounded by most of her ten children.

Susie was a "true Hutterite," according to those who knew her well. She often would admonish her fellow colony members and tried her best to teach the younger generation the true meaning of communal living.

Born in South Dakota, she lived at seven colonies in her lifetime. Having lost four young children, she was a strong, God-fearing woman.

Though harvest time was just starting for many Canadian Hutterite farmers, all work was dismissed to tend to Susie's funeral.

Her funeral was unusual in part because of the huge attendance. Usually only ministers' funerals draw such a crowd.

But the occasion was unique for another reason.

Nine years ago, in 1993, Susie's family decided she would live with her second-youngest daughter, Mary, and her husband, the Rev. Peter Hofer, at the Hillridge Colony near Cranford, Alberta. Susie's husband, Jacob, had passed on seventeen years before.

It is a common Hutterite practice for a daughter to take her parents into her home. Her colony cares for her parents' needs until their death. When the parents pass away, they are buried at the daughter's colony cemetery. Hutterites do not have family burial plots and are buried in the order of their death.

It's very rare—in fact, almost unheard of—for a colony member to have their funeral service at one colony and be buried in another.

But those were the wishes of Susie, which she made known years before her death. Similar to a will, although unwritten, her express wish was to be buried at the same colony as her late husband. Susie also chose the minister she wanted to officiate at her funeral.

The first wake was on August 13, the day of her death. Already that evening, the Hillridge Colony's large church, which could seat roughly six hundred people, was packed. Since Susie had a large family, and the Hillridge Colony is near numerous other colonies, there was a large gathering. There were people attending from across Montana and from Alberta, Saskatchewan and British Columbia.

The crowd was equally big the next day, for the second wake.

At Hutterite wakes, the people gather at the church, where the beloved who has passed on lies in a homemade oak coffin in the middle surrounded by family and friends.

The attending ministers take turns leading a song associated with death and of the beautiful place that the deceased is in. During this time, a minister will occasionally give a brief history of the person's life, the wonderful things he or she did and the examples he or she left behind for us to learn from.

The wake services start around eight and last until about midnight. Around ten o'clock coffee and sandwiches are served.

The day of Susie's funeral was a warm, peaceful day. The sun came out and dried up most of the rain that had fallen the day before. Shortly after lunch, at noon, everyone gathered at the church waiting for the eight assigned pallbearers, all of whom were Susie's grandchildren, to carry her into the church. As is Hutterite tradition, before the service starts, a group of appointed ministers goes to the family to "get their permission to take the beloved to the church."

Just as Susie had requested years before, the Rev. John Stahl of the Starland Colony officiated and the Rev. Joe Hofer of the Hodgeville Colony led the song. There were close to seven hundred people attending the service, truly a family reunion.

The caravan left around three for its destination. Upon arrival, Susie's coffin was opened for the last time for those who weren't able to attend the funeral.

Then, slowly, as the afternoon gently faded away, Susie was laid to rest in the cemetery at Mayfield Colony, just a few graves apart from her late husband, Jacob Stahl.

An Angel among Us

Seventeen months ago, God sent an angel into our lives. We cared for her needs and stood by her side, until February 16, when God opened his arms to welcome her home.

Courtney Jennifer Stahl was my only niece and the only child of my brother, Richard, and his wife, Rosa. She was born with cerebral palsy. Two weeks before her death, she was hospitalized for respiratory problems. A week later, she was diagnosed with respiratory syncytial virus, or RSV, which proved fatal.

At the time of her death, I was in Canada visiting relatives. I came home early Sunday morning with relatives on their way to the funeral. I was unable to attend the first wake Saturday night, the day she died.

In my culture, we gather in a group at the church to sing spiritual death songs for the beloved who has passed on. The songs are sung as a condolence and comfort for those who mourn. Occasionally, the minister gives a short talk, recalling the wonderful things this special child did in her short journey through this world.

All the preparations for the funeral were made Saturday afternoon, shortly after my colony learned of Courtney's death. Relatives were notified, a coffin was made and a grave was dug. Our church was set up and prepared for that evening's wake.

Activities were buzzing in the kitchen: planning and preparing meals, baking buns and setting up the dining room to feed all the people. Many people donated food and volunteered their time to help with preparing all the food that was needed.

Courtney's funeral was Monday at 12:30 at the colony's communal church. Rev. Paul Hofer (Richard's uncle) of the Elkwater Colony officiated; Rev. Paul Stahl (Rosa's uncle) of the Mayfield Colony led the song.

It amazed me how many people a small child's love could bring together. Our church was packed. Courtney was dressed in a beautiful white dress made by several colony ladies the day she died. She looked like an angel in a deep, sweet sleep, lying in her coffin.

Following the funeral, we all walked together to the colony's cemetery, where the burial took place. Rosa's three older brothers and my brother, Brian, were the pallbearers. My oldest brother, Ernie, was assigned as a pallbearer, but he sprained his ankle hurrying to be on time to carry Courtney to the church Sunday night for the wake.

As the men shoveled dirt to fill the little grave, I noticed Ernie handing the rose he carried and his crutch to a friend. Hobbling over to the grave, he grabbed a shovel to help the other men bury Courtney.

Today, as we look back over the past year, there wasn't a time when we were too tired to hold Courtney, to love her or to quiet her childish fears.

She taught us so much during the short time she was with us. She brought our family closer together. She taught us how precious life is. But the most important lesson she left behind was to live our lives in the present—not in the future, as we so often do.

The hardest part, I suppose, is glancing in her crib as we pass by, expecting to see a smiling face look back at us.

Richard and Rosa would like to thank all the doctors and nurses in Havre and Great Falls for taking such good care of Courtney. They became very attached to her and mourned her loss just as we did.

Courtney will be a memory in our hearts forever. We will never forget how she filled our hearts with love and how a single smile would light up our faces and stay with us the entire day.

We'll miss our precious little angel so much. The day Courtney went home to be with our Lord, a part of us went with her.

We're so thankful that God chose our family to care for Courtney.

Now, let us leave her to rest in peace, for we have beautiful memories in our hearts to remember her by, forever.

Hutterite Colony Shocked, Saddened by Attacks, but Still Governed by Pacifism

The colony ladies and I were busy canning fruit when we learned of the terrorist attacks in New York and Washington. We were devastated to hear that something like this could be happening in America.

In days to come, as we learned more about what actually happened, we came to realize how fortunate we are to be living in rural Montana. Since many of us probably never will get the chance to visit states like New York and Virginia, we could only imagine what the destruction of the World Trade Center and Pentagon looked like.

It hurts to hear that so many innocent fellow Americans were killed under such conditions. But beyond that, my heart goes out to all the innocent children whose lives are shattered—many who'll never see their mothers or fathers again.

In the past weeks, I've noticed and am touched by the patriotism shown throughout the United States, as well as all the fund-raising that's been going on. In all my life, I've never seen so many people suddenly show faith in God and pray.

Instead of tearing our nation apart, these terrorist attacks have actually brought us together and turned the United States into one large family, where neighbors suddenly care and help each other out.

Yet, at the same time, my earnest question is, "Why did this have to happen so people could discover they had faith and openly express it?"

We all know the United States will never be the same again, so couldn't we look beyond the point of anger, hurt and grief to see the few advantages of this event? My utmost thought is to bring the Lord's Prayer back into the American public schools.

As Hutterites, we are pacifists, which means we do not join the Army and fight.

We know that the president is facing a lot of tough decisions right now. In a way, we feel fortunate not to be in his place. Yet we respect the president for the choices he is making, because it is his duty to see what he can do within his power that's best for our country.

A friend asked me how the Hutterite society would deal with such a situation. From what's written in our sermons, the proper treatment would be to "turn the other cheek and not seek revenge."

As for the people responsible for this behavior, this is something God will deal with in His own way at the appropriate time.

Many people might see this treatment as being too lenient, so please don't be offended by what I have said, when our nation's leaders prefer to see justice done for what has happened. Our sermons also teach us that God created the governmental authority to serve for certain purposes in our country.

With the many changes that are being made, especially with our security system, we, as fellow Americans, respect those changes and will do our part to be patient and give our full cooperation. We are all proud of our country, grateful to be living in a free nation and thankful for all the personal rights and freedoms we share as American citizens.

Young First-time Blood Donor Discovers Experience is Rewarding, Not Frightening

I donated blood for the first time November 12. I was a bit nervous, but with the encouragement and approval of my mother, I decided to give it a try.

By nature, needles make me very nervous, but at the thought that a single blood donation could save a life, I quickly put my fears behind me.

Being new to the experience, I chatted with some neighboring colony friends shortly after arriving at the Van Orsdel Methodist Church in Havre.

Before long, I was ushered into line with the other donors by my grandma, who gave me a stern, yet gentle look of disapproval—as a result, I was an hour behind the rest of the ladies from my colony who had joined us for the event.

As a consequence, my grandparents left me alone to finish up while they did their shopping. I didn't mind at all, for I had just engaged in a most interesting conversation with the gentlemen next to me while I waited in line.

After being called by one of the ladies from the Red Cross team to have my blood pressure taken, I quickly discovered I was "known and recognized" by several workers on the team. When Deanna Montgomery (the lady taking my blood pressure) suggested I do my next column about blood donation, I did a quick interview with her on the spot. It turned out to be very interesting.

"Any time we have a blood drawing in a town near Hutterite colonies, there is always a great turnout," Deanna said. "It makes the day much more interesting when our blood drawings include Hutterites. Many people who don't know Hutterites think you're plain and boring, but that's not so. I enjoy the different personalities, but better yet, the added sense of humor."

As a matter of fact, thirty percent of the donors at the blood drawing in Havre that day were Hutterites, a total of thirty-four donors from five different colonies.

Out of curiosity, I asked Deanna if our blood would be shipped to New York to help the victims of the September 11 terrorist attacks. Her answer was no, because there weren't all that many survivors.

Donating blood is viewed as very important by all Hutterite colonies. My colony tries to attend all the drawings in our area if possible. We feel if we're able to give blood, for the kindness of our country and our fellow citizens, that we should give freely. According to my Uncle Paul, "If it doesn't come from the goodness of your heart, you might as well not do it."

Current Events, Election Spur Colony Discussions

When it comes to world news topics, even Hutterites like to be up to date with what's happening.

Much of the time, the source of information is hearsay—what another colony member said and what was heard from a friend from town.

But the most reliable source of information is newspapers, which the colony gets. (TVs and radios aren't allowed on a colony.)

When something does occur, the news isn't a week old or older before someone on the colony gets to hear about it.

For example, when the World Trade Center was attacked, my colony knew that same morning. A friend from town called to tell us the news.

News topics vary among genders. The guys' interest will bend more toward wheat and calf prices or events that have an impact on the market, such as the recent longshoremen dispute on the West Coast.

The search for the sniper who's responsible for the killings that took place in the East was a big news topic among the ladies.

Although the search for Osama bin Laden was of interest, it dropped out of conversation after months with no report of his arrest.

I've noticed that most of the topics that the folks at my colony keep up to date with are local Montana happenings and United States news more than world information.

At the colony school, the teacher tries to make world news a part of the students' schedule.

The election is coming up. Since most of the colony folks are registered voters, they're interested in the people running in the general election. Reading about the different candidates in the newspaper helps to prepare us when it is time to go to the polls.

The folks at my colony cast their votes in the town nearest to the colony: Gildford.

Knowing personally a person who is running in the general election makes the election even more interesting.

The teacher's aide at our colony, Kitty Galbavy-Williams, is running as a write-in candidate for Hill County Treasurer. She was the first person I've seen doing campaigning on the colony.

Who's voting for whom tends to bring up conversation topics on the colony. We like to discuss among ourselves the pros and cons of the people running. For someone who has trouble deciding which candidate would be best for the position, it helps hearing different opinions, instead of just the information we read about in the newspaper.

But in the end, each person is his or her own judge of which candidates should get his or her vote.

Voting a Novelty, Privilege

On November 7, I voted for the first time. Just turning eighteen this past July, I was new to the experience. My mom told me the basics before sending me off alone to an empty booth.

I made it through OK.

When I recently received a letter from a reader asking if Hutterites vote, I got to thinking about what an important and interesting topic it is. Many people think we don't vote. Perhaps there are many Hutterites who don't, for various reasons. They are among the forty percent of all Montanans who don't go to the polls, according to the Secretary of State's office.

Almost everyone at my colony exercises their right to vote. For those who don't, it's a personal decision, not a mandate from the colony. We don't have to seek special permission from the ministers or other elders; it's each person's individual choice.

We vote for two reasons: (1) We are United States citizens, and (2) In order to keep our public school open, we have to.

Hutterites don't get too politically involved supporting certain candidates because of lack of time and interest. However, many who have a deep interest in politics keep themselves up to date with newspaper reports and such.

The reader who wrote me this letter also was interested to learn if we pay taxes. Yes, we do. We are United States citizens; it would be illegal for us to not pay taxes. I don't know what would exclude us. After doing a little research, I learned that we pay road taxes and land taxes. We also pay taxes on our school because it is public and on colony grounds. In fact, I found we pay all kinds of county, state and federal taxes, just as you do.

Many people aren't aware that Hutterites aren't allowed to run for public office. According to our religious beliefs, to run for a public office would go against our conscience—Hutterites aren't allowed to swear on the Bible or make an oath. To make an oath means you make a promise on your life that you cannot break, and nobody can really do that.

There are a few exceptions. My dad, for example, is on our colony's school board. Instead of swearing, he "affirmed" his commitment to his new position. To affirm means that we do whatever we promise to do, to the best of our ability, and God help us.

We are allowed to get involved in the outside world only to the extent we feel is appropriate.

I learned a lot about how the election works and other political views this year because I knew it was my first time to vote. I wanted to be well aware of all the candidates' goals and promises before they get my vote.

When I dropped my form into the vote-collecting box, I was proud that I had the right and privilege to voice my opinion freely, not only as a United States citizen but also as a Hutterite.

Working Cat Becomes Stay-at-Home Mom

I'm not particularly fond of pets. In all my childhood years, I never owned a pet that I loved unconditionally or cared about enough to let it sleep at the foot of my bed. Then again, one of our household rules was no pets in the house—they shed. Mom never approved when we came home with a kitten or brought the new "cow puppy" into the house to show everyone.

Pets on a colony in most cases are only used for work. The cowboys have one or two dogs to help with the cows. Cats are used in the barns to catch mice.

Sometimes you'll find the rare exception where someone will have a personal pet for entertainment. One of my cousins has several pet peacocks and also banty chickens. Several years back he had pet rabbits. I've noticed that parrots, canaries and poodles are becoming popular in Hutterite homes.

We have a pet at our colony that's an exception, one that worked her way up from mouse cat to house cat.

Left to right: Wayne Stahl, Fred Stahl (Lisa's father), Brandon Stahl, Wesley Stahl, and Gildford Colony's herd dogs wait while the honey wagon receives the manure sludge from the fowl barn.

When my Uncle Paul got Lizzie—from who knows where—she was just a small kitten. She was solid black, except for a bit of white on her upper chest, which you could see only when you cuddled her.

The guys had a mouse problem at the shop at the time, so Paul got a cat to solve the problem. Lizzie grew up so fast, it was unbelievable. Pretty soon she had the mouse population well under control.

Lizzie has her own litter box and her own personal chair that nobody uses but her—she claimed ownership of it a while back.

Several months after moving into her new home, the shop became her territory. She patrols the area, never bothering to step out of anyone's way, in a fashion that lets you know she's "the boss." She makes her rounds several times a day, checking out what the guys are doing and seeing if the shop is still mouse-proof.

Every so often, on her way to the water bowl for a shot of cold water, she surprises one of the guys who's talking on the phone by stepping on the release button and cutting off his conversation.

When Lizzie gave birth, Uncle Paul hid the newborn felines in the shop so the kids wouldn't hurt the babies, since they couldn't walk or see yet. For about a week, the children searched the colony looking for the kittens. When they finally discovered where they were, it was Lizzie who had led them to her babies.

Of course, Lizzie got a lot of attention, now that she was a mother. Not only did the kids come visit, but our cow dog, Queenie, and Charley, a cocker spaniel who wandered around all day doing not much, also paid Lizzie several visits.

Lizzie was best friends with Charley because the two had spent many nights together at the shop. When he came to check out the new additions, he could walk up to the box, stick his nose in and smell them. Lizzie just sat there proudly, not blinking an eye.

Unfortunately, when Queenie came to check things out, all you saw was the blur of a dog running for his life for the open shop door, Lizzie not far behind.

One night, Lizzie decided to bring the kittens up to our house. Working all night, she carted each kitten from the hay bales to our porch—a good distance. My mom didn't approve of this at all. Now my little sisters spent more time with the kittens than they did doing their chores.

That day after supper, while my sisters were in town, I took the time and effort to gather the kittens in a box and take them to the barn to hide them—not so much from Lizzie as from my sisters. Of course, Lizzie found them first, and when I got up the next morning, the kittens were back under our porch.

Over the past year, I've grown fond of Lizzie. I never knew cats had their own personality and sense of humor, but Lizzie sure proved me wrong.

Feeling Bored? Use Your Imagination, the Possibilities Are Just About Endless

I have many cherished early childhood memories. For me, growing up on a colony was very exciting—there is so much to do. But most of the time our imaginations were getting us in trouble and working overtime to get us out.

Sometimes we came up with some really creative things to do— some good and some bad.

Winter seemed to be a favorite season. The best sport during recess was snowball fights. I remember we'd have two teams, and each team would have a wall of snow built up for protection. Since there were always more guys in school than girls, I normally made sure I was on a team that had most of the older boys.

Trust me, when you got hit with a snowball, you remembered it for a few days.

In the evening we'd go for sled races. During one winter, we had huge drifts in the trees that surrounded the school. Each student picked a large drift and went to work carving objects from the snow. The next day when we took the teacher to see our handiwork, she found snow caves, a huge hand and face, a bathtub, etc.

Now, the boys had their share of adventures—don't get me wrong. Whenever they were found in the act of doing something they shouldn't have, their punishment was to weed and hoe the trees that surrounded the colony grounds. By the time they graduated from school they were so good, they had our Caraganna trees clean all summer long.

At times the things we did taught us a lesson. One summer afternoon several of my cousins and I went to visit the young calves. After chasing them around in their corral and having a "rodeo," we got tired and started feeding the milk cows—which were in the adjacent corral—the calves' feed. The more we piled in front of them, the more they ate. That evening, our milk cows didn't give any milk because of our careless mistake.

When school let out, we'd gather up our camping gear and set up camp in our backyards. We'd use huge tarps or blankets to make tents and tepees. We'd swipe a dozen or so clothespins from our mothers' clotheslines to hold together our tents. Each of us brought something cold from home to eat, and we'd always make a pretend campfire.

In the fall one year, on the day before school was to start, my cousins and I went and picked every flower we could find on the colony. Then, we brought all the canning jars that we could carry home from the kitchen to make bouquets. We set the bouquets on the school porch that evening. The next day when the teacher came, she first had to make a path through the dozens of vases of flowers so she could get into the school.

Summer days were all spent outside, except for the days when it rained. Even then, my friends and I loved to race around outside getting wet.

Of course, things weren't always roses. There was the occasional fight and the "outs with each other," which never lasted more than a few hours, because it turned out not to be such a big deal after all. And if you ever ratted on your friends you earned the nickname "tattletale" for at least a week. Then you really had to get your Brownie points up before they let you back in the playgroup.

When school let out this May my sisters' first question was, "What are we going to do all summer?" I looked at them in total shock and wondered to myself, whatever happened to young children's imaginations? We never ran out of things to do.

But things are so different with kids growing up today. Many don't realize the fun of playing games besides those on computers. And climbing a tree to the top in real life instead of watching some kid do it in a magazine. Playing cops and robbers at night instead of playing Nintendo.

Of course, there's the joy of finding your first rattlesnake on the way to the dugout for a swim—after your parents gave you strict instructions not to go.

There is so much to learn and discover. There are so many questions to ask. And all you need to do is use your imagination. Sometimes that could even be scary.

Entire Family Embraces Young Visitor, Making Her Feel Right at Home

Winter is a wonderful season. It's a time to enjoy the welcome snow and watch the children make snowmen.

Since winter excuses most outdoor work for the ladies, it gives us time to catch up with the family sewing. It's also the time when the ladies go home on their "two-week winter vacation" to visit family.

When the two weeks are finished, their husbands will come to get them, usually on a weekend. That way, the kids who attend school can go along as well to visit their grandparents.

Because there is less work in winter, the young single guys get to go on a "winter trip" as well. They get to plan the trip however they want to. They usually travel to Canada and visit the colonies there, getting to know new people and places.

Our guys went on a ten-day odyssey to North Dakota, South Dakota and Minnesota this winter to visit the Schmiedeleut colonies in those states, part of a different branch of Hutterites.

I recently had the opportunity to spend a two-week vacation with my dad's sister and her family at Big Rose Colony. They live in Saskatchewan, about an hour's drive from Saskatoon.

The nearest town, Biggar (which the colony was named after), is about ten miles from the colony.

A growing town about the size of Chester, it has a population of three thousand. Proud Canadians, their town motto welcoming visitors states: "New York is Big, but this is Biggar!"

My stay at Big Rose Colony was very appealing and exciting. I was kept well-entertained by Aunt Marie's and Uncle Johnny's five children. Like my own, their home buzzes with activity every waking hour of the day.

Their second youngest, Blaine, a second-grader, was generously gifted at birth with a double shot of imagination. This winter he converted his bedroom into part schoolhouse and part greenhouse. He has a large collection of seeds, sorted and stored away for spring, to start his own vegetable and fruit garden. Whenever the family shares a fruit snack of oranges, grapefruit or apples, he's right there to collect every seed to add to his collection.

His two older brothers' imaginations, on the other hand, don't venture as far. Thirteen-year-old Ivan, who just got a permanent spot with the older boys on their hockey team (because of his swift moves and quick thinking), hopes to someday be chosen team captain.

Normally you find him with his nose stuck in a western book, unaware of what's happening around him. There is very little that worries him, and I admire his slowness to anger.

Leroy, ten, loves to work with horses and cows. His dream is to be a rancher when he grows up. By nature, he is very thoughtful and considerate of other people's needs. I often found him doing helpful things for his mother. Every night, after the evening prayer meeting, he walks his aging grandpa (the colony's oldest minister) home from church.

I enjoy their two girls, Leona, the oldest, and Kelly, the youngest, very much. Since Leona and I are the same age and share many interests, we're constantly together doing some "girl thing." She enjoys attending high school on the colony and loves horses.

Little Kelly, who turned four in December, completes the family circle. There are times when she forgets she's a girl and tries to keep up with her brother, Blaine. She'll tackle challenges that are for adults.

It's very noticeable that she's around older people a lot. A ball of energy, she keeps her family hopping and on their toes.

This wonderful family made me feel very welcome, and my vacation was well worth the time. There was never a dull or silent moment. I fit in like a perfect member of the family.

Go Ahead—Approach Hutterites with a Pleasant Greeting

You're shopping at Wal-Mart and you spot a group of Hutterites. You want to talk to them—ask them a question—but you're scared.

That's how a lot of people feel. They're not sure how to interact with Hutterites when they see them in public.

They're not sure how they'll respond.

They might be shy like you, since they've lived on the colony all their lives and have had only a few experiences with outsiders. They might be a little held-back when it comes to talking to a stranger.

Then there are others who are just the opposite: talkative, easy-going and eager to share the conversation.

For Hutterites, good public relations are important. Colony people have to deal with the public (known as "English people" in German) on a daily basis.

Whatever cannot be raised and manufactured on the colony has to be bought. Colony folks constantly interact with businesspeople at parts stores, grocery stores, large implement dealers and veterinary offices. We often deal with pork and beef salesmen.

When a new colony is established, colony people get to know their neighbors.

They work and grow with them through the years. They are there to help one another out in an emergency and to lend a helping hand during calving, branding, cattle shipping, seeding and harvest time.

They are constantly borrowing tools and equipment from one another.

Often a colony's garage is a repair center, where a neighbor will stop by to do repairs on a tractor or fix a flat tire.

But interacting means a lot more than work. It includes developing friendships that last for years, and eventually a lifetime.

Visits to the colony are frequent. There are few days when meals are eaten at the communal kitchen that an English friend isn't there to join in.

On a lazy summer evening, you'll likely find a couple of the guys going fishing with a friend. Or on a Sunday afternoon, a family from town will come out to the colony to spend the day with friends.

When a colony has a celebration—a wedding, shivaree, harvest party, Christmas or graduation program—it's the perfect chance for neighbors and friends to gather and share the evening.

Events like these are a chance for the colonies to get together with their English friends and neighbors.

It's important to have good communication among the neighbors.

In the last decade, more Hutterites started volunteering for their local fire departments. Others, women as well as men, have joined the ambulance team and trained to become first responders.

Colony tours are frequent and can range from one person to a group of one hundred. People touring the colony come from all over the United States, as well as other parts of the world.

On tours, people who have never visited a colony get to see how such a large organization works, and also ask questions. A lot of times, it's a chance to clear up some of the misunderstandings they may have about Hutterites and colony life.

So next time you're shopping at Wal-Mart or Sam's Club and you see a Hutterite, take a chance to say "Hi" or ask a question.

There's a chance the results will be rewarding.

The Paul Stahl, Jr., family, encompassing four generations, comes together for a barbecue.

Holidays and Celebrations

෴

Halloween? It's All About the Candy

I smiled at the sight of my three little sisters emptying out their Halloween bags into a large fruit bowl and sorting their treats in piles on the sitting room floor. The bubble gum in one pile, suckers in another, bars in another . . .

It reminded me of when I was their age. I would do the same thing when I'd come home from trick-or-treating. My brothers and I would put all our candy in the same bowl and when no one was looking, I'd go through the bowl and pick out the best stuff and secretly hide it in my bedroom. That way, my older brothers wouldn't always get the better end.

Although we enjoy October 31 as children, Halloween in our culture is celebrated a bit differently than traditional America celebrates it.

To us, it isn't about ghosts and goblins. It isn't about dressing up as a witch or painting our faces and hair. No, it's not about decorating a neighbor's tree with toilet paper because we didn't get a treat.

Halloween to us is about getting candy. Simple as that! It is the only day of the year we can go from house to house and get candy for no reason at all. And it is probably the only day we can get a bad stomachache from having too many sweets.

For us, Halloween is a quiet holiday. It's about seeing the joy and happiness on the children's faces when they get their treats. It's also about kids getting the treats and not teenagers and grownups.

We only go for treats around the colony, so the ladies make the event special. They make small bags of candy for each child, using a variety of candy, with creative choices.

Right after supper, the kids gather as a group at one of their houses and decide when they are going to start. With the older kids holding the younger kids' hands, they start their rounds. None of their faces are painted, and their costumes consist of a jacket and mittens over their school clothes, to keep warm.

They know at each house a special treat awaits them. They also know if someone doesn't give them a treat, they won't play a trick on them, because there is probably a good reason behind the lack of a treat.

To our kids, Halloween could be any day of the year. To them, it's not important which day it is, what it's called or how the world celebrates it. What's important is making sure they get their bag of treats!

Hutterites Offer Thanks for Harvest, Good Friends

Thanksgiving is observed by Hutterites each year. There's the usual big turkey, stuffing and the trimmings that go along with the Thanksgiving meal.

Our colony did something different this year: We combined Thanksgiving with our harvest party.

The colony's harvest didn't take very long this year—about three weeks. But after the guys were done cutting our crop, they took on several custom-cutting jobs, and because of that we had to push our harvest party into November. Since it ended up being so close to Thanksgiving, we decided to combine the two occasions.

Most Hutterite colonies have harvest parties, known as "Hachinka." The party represents thanks given for that year's harvest.

The harvest party was very special to us this year, because we didn't have one for four years because harvest was not very good.

The celebration started Wednesday at six o'clock in the evening and was a pleasant evening of food, friends, fun and entertainment.

The food was set up buffet style. Each year, the menu varies. This year, the cooks were busy preparing breaded shrimp, spare ribs and hot wings, as well as several side dishes. For dessert, there was fruit pizza.

The invited guests were many longtime neighbors and friends from town, as well as implement dealers, salesmen and ranchers with whom the men had worked throughout the summer when trying to get the crop in. Many of the neighbors are people we share tools with.

Unlike regular mealtime, when women sit separately from the men, at the harvest party everyone is free to sit where they wish and mingle with the crowd.

As supper came to an end, the young girls sang several songs they'd been practicing for the occasion.

Then out of the crowd popped one of the guys with a "surprise package" wrapped in layers and layers of newspaper. On each sheet there was a joke, addressed specifically to a colony member. When the last piece of newspaper was peeled away, the crowd was eager to learn the surprise inside—this year's was a small bride doll, given in jest to one of the single guys.

When the last guest was done eating and the last sound of laughter died away into the late night, all the guests and colony members joined together to clean up the dining room and wash the dishes.

The night is a pleasant memory of the thankful things God did for us throughout the summer. And each year, it's a wonderful feeling to be able to share an evening of thanksgiving with our friends and neighbors, not as a colony, but as a family.

Despite Dry Year, Colony Has Lots to be Thankful For

It's been a pleasant Thanksgiving weekend.

Every year during the week of Thanksgiving my colony makes

our winter supply of Saturday sausage. The men and ladies did this at the beginning of the week, and the project took two full days. But it was all worth the effort on Wednesday, when we served the freshly smoked sausage for supper for the first time.

Thanksgiving Day is very busy preparing for the big supper. The ladies start preparations a day ahead of time, cutting up the vegetables for the stuffing,

My sister-in-law, Rosa, and I cooked the Thanksgiving meal this year, because Thanksgiving was in our cook week. We got up earlier than usual to start preparing the two large turkeys. My mom, who is the head cook, prepared the stuffing by frying it first, then adding all the seasonings. She put it into pans to bake later that afternoon.

Rosa and I cooked two types of cranberries—one to eat with the turkey meat and the other to serve with the ice cream. A lady friend from town, who joined us for supper with her husband, generously offered to make a pumpkin dessert, which we also served with the meal. We also served potatoes and a gravy made from the turkey broth.

Pumpkin pie is another big Thanksgiving tradition for us. The lady baking this week made the pie on Wednesday and divided it among all the colony members to eat at home as a snack.

For the kids, it was a long weekend. They had school off from Thursday through Sunday, but still attended a morning and afternoon class of German school. Some of the parents took their kids to visit their grandparents at other colonies during the long break.

My fondest Thanksgiving memory from growing up on the colony is attending German school on Thanksgiving Day. Our German schoolteacher asked us to write a full-page report of what we were thankful for in German. (If we wrote it in English, which we tried, he made us redo it.) Then we had to go to the front of the class and read it aloud.

Several years back, the young girls set up a Thanksgiving display on hay bales in the kitchen. We decorated it with wheat and brought up from the root cellar our biggest pumpkin, squash, potatoes, zucchini and other garden vegetables. It was a beautiful scene of Thanksgiving for what the Lord had given us that year. Because of the dry summer, we weren't able to make a similar display this year.

But still, we have a lot to be thankful for. God is always watching over us and looking out for our needs. I'm thankful to have my family close by, grateful to live in a free country and privileged to be living the life God chose for me.

Christmas is Goodies and Gifts, but Mostly Christ

In my culture, Christmas is one of the biggest spiritual holidays we celebrate and probably by far the most important. But the way we celebrate Christmas is a lot different than how the general public celebrates it.

Just like each nationality has its tradition of celebrating Christmas, so do the Hutterites.

Food is a good example. Each year, two different ladies get to pick six kinds of Christmas cookies to bake. All the ladies join in making the cookies, which are then divided equally among each of the colony members.

A month before Christmas, the famous "Saturday Sausage" is made and is scheduled on the menu each Saturday for lunch.

One of the biggest Christmas treats is "nicklus." It's a large variety of bars, candy, gum, chips, crackers, nuts and dried fruit, which is given to each family a few weeks before Christmas as a gift from the colony.

During the week of Christmas and New Year's, the colony will plan special meals. For example, on Christmas Eve, we'll have turkey and stuffing. For supper on Christmas Day, the cooks will make plates of "Surprise Spread."

Christmas decorations are frowned upon and are rarely seen in Hutterite homes. In an older couple's home, you probably won't see more than a string of Christmas cards hanging from one wall to another.

Sending Christmas cards is something everyone seems to do a lot of. Many times with families with younger children, it's a game to see who gets the most cards.

Of course, exchanging Christmas gifts is something that is not frowned upon. This part of Christmas is very special for the children.

Everyone will gather with their own families for gift exchanging, which usually happens on Christmas Eve. Many times, in large families, names are drawn for the exchange and price limits are set.

Exchanging gifts among dating couples is a highlight of the season. Special Christmas cards are bought, and gifts are chosen with extra care. It's always a treat to be able to spend Christmas with the one you love.

The children's Christmas program is a special night for a Hutterite colony, as well as the surrounding neighbors who are asked to attend the occasion. The students' parents make special treats, which are shared with all in attendance following the program.

But by far the most important are the church sermons we have during Christmas break. We have services December 25, 26 and 27, and again on New Year's Day and January 6.

Each year, the story of the birth of Christ is respoken, yet the goodness of it never seems to fade away. How many of us are there who are able to celebrate this beautiful season with our families and in peace?

Even though we get to celebrate the birth of Christ year after year, in our hearts, it is something we should never take for granted.

This Christmas Bound To Be Extra Special

My three younger sisters ran home from the evening rehearsal at the church, where they met with the other colony kids to recite their plays for Thursday's Christmas program.

"Mom, I'm a boy," Gloria announced upon entering the house. "None of the boys in school wanted to be the main male actor in one of the plays, so I volunteered—and I got it!"

"And I'm the narrator," said Rhoda, in a fake grownup voice. A fourth-grader this year and the youngest in our family, she'd easily won the important role, as she is mature for a girl her age and quick to take on big responsibilities.

In a rush of mixed English and German, they quickly supplied my mother with an idea of what to expect on their big show night. They were cautious, though, so as not to give away any surprises.

"We're adding a touch of patriotism this year, too," added Lorraine, the oldest of the three. "We want to do something to show our respect for our country for what's been happening in the past few months."

Christmas is a very exciting time for young Hutterite children. They have so many activities going on that they're kept extra busy throughout the month of December. Besides their program plays and songs, they're practicing songs they'll sing on their caroling rounds at each colony home the evening of the 25th. As it comes closer to the program, the older schoolgirls will add a helping hand making special holiday treats for everyone to share afterward at the communal kitchen.

Doing a little spy work, with the thought of helping out "the guy up north," I asked my sisters what they were going to tell Santa their Christmas wishes were this year. After much consideration, my sister Gloria replied, "There's a lot of stuff I want—an umbrella, a diary, a pet puppy—but do you know what I'd really wish for? I wish that all the people in the world would get along and be friends."

Her answer greatly surprised me, for I was expecting a long list of impossibilities. Yet it dawned on me that if I had my wish, similar to my sister's, I too would wish for world peace—and two feet of beautiful, wet snow.

In my culture, we exchange gifts each Christmas, but we don't go to extremes. We try not to hide the true meaning of Christmas behind a pile of gifts, decorated trees and walls. We must all remember that the real reason for this special celebration is the birth of baby Jesus, born in a manger in Bethlehem long, long ago.

Of all the past Christmases I've celebrated with my family, I strongly feel in my heart that this year will be one of the most special and remembered Christmases ever. After all that has happened in the past few months, I think Christmas will bring every American family closer, so as not to take for granted what's so special about this Christian holiday.

Christmas a Time for Jesus, Loved Ones, and the Long-Awaited Christmas Program

Walking home from a neighbor's house, I spotted the school kids on their way to the communal church for rehearsal for their annual Christmas program.

They've been practicing extra hard this week, memorizing their lines and perfecting their acting skills. I write in anticipation of this year's December 21 performance. Just watching the kids hurry to rehearsal, lugging along their props, makes you catch the Christmas spirit.

Their guests will consist of all the colony members, many of the local neighbors and a few people from town.

Featured this year are two plays, "The Fourth Wise Man" and "The Christmas Miracle of Jonathan Toomey." At least that's what I've gathered from the photocopied scripts I peeped at, found while tidying up our house, and from bits and pieces of other stuff my sisters just couldn't help but share excitedly with my mom and me when they came home from school.

Of course, we have to remind them that it's really supposed to be a secret, and they hold their breath, suddenly remembering the same thing.

As is custom, front seats are reserved for the performers' parents. The program normally lasts an hour. Concluding the presentation is a visit from Santa, all dressed in red with his curly white beard.

Later, there is a snack party at the kitchen put on by students and their parents.

The Christmas program is an event many of our neighbors look forward to because it gives them a chance to come visit their friends here at our colony. It's a great get-together for everyone attending.

Christmas Eve is family time for everyone—sharing the evening with loved ones, singing praise to the birth of our Savior and the opening of presents.

Christmas Day starts with a beautiful church service, retelling the famous story of the birth of Jesus so long ago. That afternoon at Sunday school, the nonbaptized members of the colony recite about ten German Christmas songs and later are rewarded with a package of candy (as in an old tradition) from the colony's boss.

We also have church services on December 26 and 27.

On the evening of Christmas Day, I hope to take the school-aged kids and some of the younger ones caroling to all the colony homes.

At each home they'll first sing a well-known German Christmas song, then take requests for English Christmas songs.

What a wonderful holiday Christmas is! I hope everyone can spend Christmas with a joyous heart and in good spirits this year. But most of all, the best part of Christmas is being able to spend it with your family and those you love. And let's not forget the true reason why we celebrate this holiday—the birth of Jesus Christ, born to the Virgin Mary many years ago in a faraway town called Bethlehem. That's why this beautiful holiday is called CHRISTmas!

Church, Family, Little Children All Part of Special Christmastime on Colony

Tomorrow is the last day of the year. It's so hard to believe how fast time goes by. If we don't watch out and enjoy life's precious moments, we'll miss them completely.

What a beautiful, memorable Christmas my family had this year! I tried to be a part of all the activities that were going on in my culture, so I wouldn't miss any, and so the memory of this Christmas would stay with me always.

Christmas Eve at my colony was spent in our homes, opening gifts with our families. Though the children received the most gifts, many of the adults had drawn names earlier that month and exchanged gifts. We do this as individual families; it isn't an entire colony matter.

For supper on Christmas Eve we had turkey, stuffing and the trimmings. Everyone was dressed in their Sunday best, and all the ladies had on a new dress they'd made special for the occasion.

Christmas Day was a quiet, peaceful, snowless day spent together with our families. We had a morning church service regarding the birth of baby Jesus. The story was read from Luke 2.

Christmas Day was a special time for the children. Shortly after lunch, the preschoolers stood in line in the kitchen and recited the German songs they'd been learning in their preschool classes. Their audience included all their teachers, their parents and grandparents and many other colony members. Afterward, the colony boss and several older colony ladies who teach preschool presented each child with a bag of candy.

That afternoon at Sunday school, the school-aged children and non-baptized adults also recited several songs in German. When we were finished, the German schoolteacher and the colony's boss explained the importance and meaning of the songs and why we memorize them. They reminded us of important youth duties, such as taking time to read the Bible, memorizing our verses in the evening and doing good things for the colony and its members. Later, we, too, were presented with a bag of candy for our effort, an old tradition.

My colony also had church services on December 26 and 27, as all Hutterites do. The families on the colony spend the Christmas holidays together, sharing each other's time and company. We do things together such as singing German Christmas songs and going to other homes to visit. Some parents went to other colonies with their children to visit their relatives during the holiday break.

We also will have a church service on Tuesday. This service is about hailing the new year. It also pertains to the day that Jesus was given his name. We have our last Christmas service on Sunday, telling the story of the three wise men.

I'm so happy that I could celebrate Jesus' birth with my family. I feel sorry for those who can't be with their families at Christmas. It makes Christmas so much more special because in my culture, family is everything.

Baptism a Somber and Heartfelt Affair Involving Entire Community

Four young members of my community are getting baptized this Easter.

For the past seven weeks, they've been going through classes taught by the elders of our colony.

Classes begin nine weeks before Easter. The year before, those who wish to be baptized make their wishes known. For that year, they must show they are in earnest, for instance, by attending church regularly.

On the Sunday before classes, each person who has made the decision to be baptized and become a brother or sister of the church goes to the German schoolteacher to ask for help and guidance.

The teacher explains the procedure to them, what they will have to give up and that they have to become more obedient to the community.

When the teacher is finished, he tells them to go to the eldest minister to ask for his help as well.

If the eldest minister accepts their proposal, he informs the group that, at the evening prayer, all the brothers of the church will vote to accept or deny their proposal to become baptized.

Sometimes they are accepted, and sometimes they aren't, depending upon their behavior the year before. If they're accepted, they begin classes the following Sunday. Around one o'clock in the afternoon, they start their rounds, in which they go to each member of the church council, by the order of their position in the colony—ministers first, and then to the boss and so on.

Each Sunday, after they enter each elder's home, they recite a small poem, "My dear brother, we have a heartfelt request, with God and all holy, a promise to uphold, and we ask you to help us, with the help of God."

During the seven weeks, they also learn two other poems that they'll recite in front of the community the day before they are baptized. The first is a series of questions asked about their belief and faith. The second is a long poem asking God to help them in making such a lifelong decision.

On Saturday of the eighth week, we have church in the afternoon for the baptizers, as they are then called. They sit in their usual seats, and when the ministers are ready, they ask them to come to the front of the church to recite their poems.

When they are finished, once again, each member of the council will give them an encouraging word.

The big day is Sunday. Church starts at nine in the morning, as usual. Around ten, the baptizers get baptized in the presence of their family and friends and the entire community.

The guys wear a long black church jacket (also known as a minister's jacket) that reaches to their knees. The girls wear a black dress made of special material, sometimes satin.

Starting with the oldest, the minister lays his hands on the head of a baptizer and the second minister pours water from a china jar on the person's head while they kneel. Then the oldest minister gives the person a baptism blessing, shakes his right hand and says, "May God strengthen you." In return, the new brother or sister says, "May God be with us."

Then they shake hands with all the brothers and sisters and repeat the sayings.

The decision to become baptized is a choice each person must make on his own when he is of age—anytime after age nineteen. It is not a forced decision—some Hutterites choose not to be baptized, and some wait until after they are thirty, although Hutterites must be baptized before they can get married. We do not get baptized as babies because we believe a child cannot acknowledge and understand what baptism is.

What does baptism mean to a Hutterite today? A lot. They know that when they see their neighbor doing something wrong, that they must admonish them, but also must learn to be admonished in return.

They know they must surrender, totally and completely, to God, to accept Him as their personal savior, to become born again.

Traditions Make Easter Extra Special

Easter is one of the most important holidays in my culture. This year, with the added baptism events, it made the holiday even bigger and more special.

The baptism events passed too quickly, but beautifully. The four young people who were baptized did an excellent job of reciting their two poems. Even though they were under pressure from reciting in front of the entire community, they didn't make a single mistake.

The week of Easter itself is very busy and full of activities, spiritual as well as cultural. To start off the holiday, we always bake our traditional Orange Fruit Cake, which we only make at Easter.

Our church services begin on Good Friday. As I mentioned in my last column, we had the baptism church services the Saturday and Sunday before Easter.

Easter Sunday, there are two services—one in the morning and one in mid-afternoon. For Easter, we usually prepare an extra-special dish called "Surprise Spread." It's a cold dish we serve at supper, made up of a whipping of sour cream, cream cheese and mayonnaise, spread on a plate. Then we spread seafood cocktail on top of that, sprinkle mozzarella cheese, green peppers, tomatoes and shrimp, and eat it with crackers.

Sometime during the week, the children paint eggs with their parents or grandparents, and each family has its own Easter egg hunt on Sunday. To add good spirits to the holiday, the cooks take the time to paint eggs as well, which they serve at breakfast on Sunday.

The Monday after Easter is also a very important holiday. This is the day when all the baptized members of the church (all the brothers and sisters) take communion—in German known as Abendmahl. We only take the communion once a year, always on the Monday after Easter Sunday.

The Abendmahl church service normally lasts three hours. Sometime toward the end of the service, the minister passes around the bread, baked the previous day by his wife. Everyone breaks off a piece and eats it. He also passes around a jar of wine for everyone to take a sip. The bread represents Jesus' body and the wine His blood.

During church, it's the responsibility of the adult girls who aren't baptized yet to cook the noon meal. They also make the traditional Easter cream puffs, which are a favorite of everybody. At lunch, everyone adds ice cream to the puff and eats it for dessert.

Since the adult girls are occupied with cooking (and answering the phone, as it's a tradition among the young people to call their friends during church Monday), several of the younger girls are in charge of babysitting the other colony children.

As for the guys, well, you can guess what they do. During church, they'll come to the kitchen to bother and tease the cooks, and when we're not looking, they'll each swipe a few cream puffs before leaving.

We have our last Easter service on Tuesday. The service is earlier than usual, so the kids can attend school that day.

My family had a "special" guest staying with us for the Easter holidays. My mother's brother, Uncle Joe, from Alberta, spent the past two weeks with us. Joe is special to my family for several reasons. With a tossed kiss or a simple smile, he can win your heart over in a second. He's the only person who calls me by my full name, though it sounds more like, "Lita Ma-we."

Each member of my family looks forward to spending time with Joe. He has a special place in our hearts and lives. Even though my Uncle Joe is mentally handicapped, it doesn't stop us from loving him even more.

He reminds us of the importance of a holiday like Easter—to celebrate its significance and understand our cultural religious holidays. He also teaches us to strive and learn from today, before moving on to tomorrow.

Oh, Get Ready; There's Going To Be a Wedding

Today my youngest brother, Richard, is getting married. He's the first from our family to marry, so we are sort of new to all the immediate family tasks that need to be done in the wedding preparations.

We've been planning for this wedding for a whole year now. And we didn't start a bit too early, either.

Throughout the spring and summer, my mom and I worked at making all the wedding clothes needed for each member of our family.

The bride is Rosa Stahl, from the Mayfield Colony at Etzikom, Alberta.

She has been just as busy preparing for her wedding as we've been. The bride's preparation in a wedding is much bigger than the groom's. Since the bride moves to the groom's colony, she has to make special plans ahead of time of how she wants her new home furnished, how she wants her colors to be and so much more.

Rosa's wedding colors are peach and white—a perfect fall combination. Her wedding cake turned out exactly the way we had planned, along with her bouquet and other accessories.

As is our tradition, the procedure started the Sunday before. My brother asked the other male baptized members of the church for guidance with the spiritual requirements of his attempt to be joined in marriage. They accepted his proposal and offered their help.

Thursday afternoon, he proudly left for Canada in the company of my dad and his two older brothers. That evening, in the presence of her entire family, friends and neighboring relatives, my brother asked for Rosa's hand in marriage. It's a sad and emotional event—giving away a beloved daughter.

The next evening, Rosa's colony was the host for a big supper and shivaree, a wedding celebration. At the shivaree, different colony choirs and soloists sang hymns and German wedding songs. They also had a big evening snack, and some of the youth performed skits.

Late that evening, Rosa and Richard went to each home at her colony to bid each family farewell. This is the most emotional part of the wedding ceremony for the bride.

The wedding caravan left for Montana right after breakfast Saturday morning. When they arrived at our colony just before noon, they were greeted with signs along the way welcoming the couple home. On the back of a decorated pickup were the children and girls holding balloons. The driver led the wedding party into the colony and to the groom's parents' home.

There, the couple was greeted by my family and the rest of our colony. That evening, my colony was the host for a shivaree party. The Gildford Colony Youth Choir (our school-aged kids and some younger) brought some good-natured fun to the celebration with a group song they had been practicing for the past two months.

Carrying real roses and candles, they sang "Diesel Ford," a spoof on the biblical wedding song "Camel Train," about Isaac's father sending his slaves to a foreign land to find a bride for Jacob. In this case, the camels and biblical names were replaced with a farm truck and the names of my father and brothers.

My three little sisters also sang a humorous song they put words to called "Oh, Where Have You Been, Richard Boy?"

Today is the big day. The church service starts at nine this morning. Around ten, Richard and Rosa will exchange wedding vows in the presence of all their family, friends and relatives. Later, they will enjoy a vast dinner in the communal kitchen.

And as the day draws to a close, it will leave everyone tired but filled with the joy and happiness they were able to share with the couple.

Hutterites from other colonies propose a toast to Ben Tschetter and Lisa Marie Stahl, soon to be married.

As for the couple, they are left with treasured memories of everyone who helped make their wedding day so special.

Hutterite Wedding Still Follows a Lot of Traditional Steps, but Times Change

When I was in the eighth grade, I wrote a short nonfiction story for a school project about a wedding in a Hutterite community.

I spent many long hours doing research to get all of my information and translations correct, all on a paper about a wedding that took place in a culture and community in which I was born and raised. I had attended many weddings and thought I was familiar with all the steps and procedures, but when it came time for me to put them down on paper, I found myself coming up with a lot of blanks.

My research project took me to my parents and other older colony members, such as the ministers who perform the marriage. When my story was finished, I couldn't believe how much I had accomplished and learned through the experience. I couldn't believe how many things I didn't know, because I had never given it much thought.

Four years later, some parts of my manuscript would be invalid. Many changes have been made in the past few years concerning a Hutterite wedding. Many new "traditions" have been started and old traditions forgotten.

Marriage is a very important step a person takes as a Hutterite, for several reasons. It's a step taken when a person is mature of age, somewhere from twenty and older. A person has to be baptized before he or she can get married. The choice that is made is always definite, because divorces aren't allowed.

Marriages in Hutterite colonies aren't arranged, although it might have been that they were about a century ago. No one is pressured into getting married, and the choice is a personal one. Some Hutterites choose to remain single.

About a decade ago, a Hutterite wedding lasted five days—Wednesday through Sunday. In the past few years they've been cut back to three or four days.

Thursday or Friday, the groom goes to the bride's colony to aufred—to ask the bride's parents and family for her hand in marriage. That evening the bride's colony has a huge supper and a shivaree—a celebration where everyone gathers in one home to visit and sing love songs.

Saturday, the bride and groom (along with the bride's family, friends and other wedding guests) travel to the groom's colony. That evening the groom's colony has a supper and shivaree. The wedding takes place at the groom's colony because that is where the bride's new home will be.

Ahead of time, a home is prepared and furnished for the couple by the groom's colony.

Sunday morning, around ten o'clock, they exchange wedding vows. The bride wears a traditional royal blue satin dress. The groom wears a white shirt and black dress pants, accompanied by a jacket that reaches to his knees and is parted in the lower back. This type of jacket is only worn when a young man is baptized or married. However, since ministers wear these jackets to church, they are referred to as a "minister's jacket."

A wedding is much more complicated than I have described. It takes months and even years to prepare. In the end, it's a union of two people's lives that is worked on for a long time with tender loving care.

It's a weekend of joyous memories to look back on and a future of happiness to look forward to.

Baptism and Marriage are Newest Path for Columnist

Many of you might not find this the nicest New Year's greeting from me, but I do hope that deep down you are happy with the news I'm about to share.

Along life's way many of us find a different path to walk upon. I have found mine.

In January, the Great Falls Tribune will publish my last "On the Colony" column. I have chosen to quit my column for good because of two important steps I'm about to take in my life.

The first is baptism. I've come to make a sincere decision to dedicate my life to God and become a "sister" of my church.

In the Hutterite church, baptism is a conscious step that is always taken as an adult. The decision is one's own and is made by those nineteen and older. No one is pressured to be baptized, and some Hutterites choose not to. Some wait until they're in their thirties.

Baptism is required before marriage.

My seven weeks of pre-baptism classes will start in February. During this time, I am to follow certain rules that will show I'm in earnest about my decision. Those rules include never missing a single attendance of the evening prayer, church on Sunday morning or a meal at the communal kitchen.

I'm also required to learn two poems, which I'll recite a week before Easter, on a Saturday.

Each Sunday afternoon during my seven weeks of classes, when I'll make my rounds to all the elders on the church council, I'll be wearing a black dress made especially for the occasion. At the weekly classes, I'll learn the true meaning of Hutterite adult baptism and why it's so important to take the event seriously.

I'll be baptized the Sunday before Easter. My family will attend the ceremony with the entire congregation.

The next important step in my life, which I plan on taking sometime later in the year, is marriage. In my next column I'd like to share with you the preparations of a Hutterite wedding.

So my dear friends, I hope you aren't saddened by my decision, but find this time in my life a new beginning, filled with excitement and adventure.

Young Couple Begins Preparations for Upcoming Wedding

Two weeks ago, I shared the news with my readers that I was quitting my column for good in January because of two important events that will take place in my life.

Lisa Marie Stahl and Ben Tschetter share a romantic moment
by the stock pond when he comes to Gildford Colony for a visit.

Before Easter, in April, I'll be baptized and will become a "sister" of our church.

Then, later in the year, I'm getting married. The groom is Ben Tschetter of the Estuary Colony in Leader, Saskatchewan, which will be my new home. We met more than four years ago, when I attended his brother's wedding, and we were engaged in April 2001.

Supportive Mate

Ben has been supportive of my column over the years. He was very disappointed when I shared the news of quitting my column in January.

He has a personal collection of all my columns, which he updates on each visit to Montana. He also has me make him copies of all the letters I get from readers, which he collects as well.

The decision to quit my column was one I made alone. It's a decision I'm happy with because of the important (and big) steps I'm taking in life. But at the same time, I feel a wave of sadness fall over me to leave something this big behind, because I see my column as a necessary service to Montana.

We haven't set a wedding date yet, but we've already started preparations.

Choosing furniture and other household necessities is important and is done beforehand. When a young woman gets baptized, she gets certain pieces of furniture from her colony, which will be part of her new home when she marries. Things are different for the guys. Men get a set of furniture after they marry, such as a bedroom suite, kitchen and sitting room furnishings.

It's customary in Hutterite culture for the bride to sew the wedding clothes for herself, her family and the groom. Since I have a family of eight, I'm getting an early start.

Sewing Up a Storm

Since Hutterite weddings last four days, I need to make at least three different sets of clothes for each person. Satin is common for brides to wear, but not the wedding guests. I'll wear a different color for each day, with royal blue reserved for Sunday, the day of the wedding.

The groom has special clothes to wear as well. He'll wear a different white cotton shirt each evening. He'll wear a "minister's coat," a long dress jacket that parts in the back, to church on Sunday. A man wears this jacket only twice in his lifetime, when he is baptized and on his wedding day.

I'm not left alone with all the preparations. My immediate family, aunts, cousins and best friends are all happy to have a part in making our big day special.

As is Hutterite custom, after baptism and Easter, Ben will go to the minister of his colony to ask for a home. We have no worries about having a place to live because his colony will provide the furnished home as a wedding gift.

With an estimated time of when our new home will be finished, we'll be able to set a wedding date.

A few weeks before the wedding, several close friends will come to help me pack all of my belongings and prepare me for the move to my new home in Canada. It is customary for a Hutterite woman to join her husband's colony.

Hutterite weddings are always held on Sunday.

Wedding Week

On Monday afternoon the week of the wedding, I'll have a tea party or bridal shower for all the colony ladies at my home.

On Thursday the preparations will begin, such as setting up the dining room in the communal kitchen. Sometime that afternoon, the long wait will end when Ben, his dad and a brother will arrive at my colony.

After their arrival, a meeting with all the baptized male members of the colony will be called. At the meeting the minister will announce the groom's request for marriage and will ask if anyone objects.

Shortly after the meeting, there will be a gathering at the bride's home for yet another important tradition, asking for the bride's hand in marriage. Each family member will be given the chance to state their opinion, starting with the bride's father and mother. This process usually lasts about an hour.

Following this gathering is the evening prayer meeting where the bride and groom will rehearse their wedding vows.

On Thursday night, an evening celebration known as a shivaree is held at the bride's colony. At the shivaree, German and English wedding songs are sung, snacks are served and the guests socialize.

On Friday or Saturday, the wedding party leaves for its appointed destination—the groom's colony where yet another shivaree takes place that evening.

Emotional Goodbye

But before the wedding party leaves, another special event takes place for the bride.

With the groom at her side, she visits all the homes at her colony to bid everyone farewell. This is a very emotional event for the young woman, because she is leaving behind her family and friends and the only place she has ever called home.

The big day is Sunday. Church starts at nine in the morning. Around ten, the couple exchanges their wedding vows in the presence of God, their family and friends.

Church is followed by a big lunch, and at three o'clock a snack is served in the kitchen. The last part of the wedding is supper.

I know things will be different at my new home, but still, I'm looking forward to the change. Yet I strongly feel that no matter where I'll be, I'll always have a piece of Montana in my heart. But of course, I won't be alone; I'll have someone special to spend my tomorrows with.

Some of the men bring a small herd of cattle down from the hills for the annual branding at Kilby Butte Colony.

Farming and Nature

❦

Spring a Delightful Time of Happiness, Hope on Colony

I love spring—it's my favorite season. It's the most beautiful time of year, when all creation comes to life again. I love to watch the robins outside our kitchen window play with each other. I enjoy watching as our trees' buds turn into leaves and the grass changes color.

When I go for walks in the evening around our farm, I watch for the Canadian geese on our straw bales, where they have their nests. Each year the same pairs come back to nest here, and out of respect for nature, the guys work around certain bales, leaving them undisturbed where protective mothers sit and guard their eggs.

Our annual supply of ducklings and goslings arrived at the local post office sometime in the middle of May.

They're taken care of by my dad, the colony's poultry man. The kids are at the barn visiting them daily, eager to hold their little yellow fuzzy bodies.

Each morning our class of Little Schoolers (from ages three to five, taught by several colony ladies) urges their teacher to take them to the barn so they can play with the little critters.

The school kids are counting down the days to when school will be dismissed and summer break begins. They're already making plans for how they'll be spending their summer, the friends they'll be visiting and the fun they'll have. Right now, they're also making arrangements for where they'll be going for their annual end-of-the-year field trip.

From what I've gathered from my sisters, they're also planning a big surprise for the parents at school to present to them just a few days before school lets out.

Shortly after the Easter holiday, the men did the annual spring seeding. The event took less than two weeks, as always.

They tried something new this year—they seeded with the help of a demo Global Positioning System. It's a device that's guided by satellite, that helps farmers seed in a straight line, as well as make sure they don't overlap and double seed an area.

This device was tried simply out of curiosity, but it might find its way into Hutterite seeding operations permanently in the future. From bits and pieces of conversation, the guys find the GPS technology very pleasing and impressive.

Our gardener also is finished seeding the communal garden. He planted all the vegetables that are normally planted, in their same amounts. The only exception this year was not setting up the garden's irrigation pipes, because with our dugout dry, there is no water to irrigate with.

Even though this winter we didn't have a lot of moisture, we are hoping spring rains will make up for it. We welcome every drop of rain we've received but are saddened at the sight of the strong prairie winds blowing it all away.

It's not up to us to decide whether this year will be a dry year or not. We must not lose faith in God, and we pray that it will eventually rain. We must be patient, wait and hope for a positive outcome. As the old adage goes, every gray cloud has a silver lining.

Colonies Embrace GPS Technology for Seeding

With solemn attitudes and silent determination, the men at Gildford Colony spread their sixty-foot Flexi-coil air seeders—pulled by a versatile 976 Ford tractor—over the barren fields to begin seeding Monday morning.

The previous week's twenty-two to thirty-three mile-per-hour winds evaporated even more moisture available for spring seeding. Several of our men spent a day pushing away a foot of topsoil, which had blown and embedded in the caragana trees surrounding our colony.

Even though the colony has slowly changed to modern seeding techniques, they will do little to improve the drought condition.

The colony approves of most advanced technology that will help us stay afloat in today's competitive farm and ranch industry. It is adopted only if it is a benefit and advantage to the colony.

The men were introduced to Global Positioning System satellite technology at the farm and agriculture meetings they attend in Havre, Great Falls and in Canada.

Last fall, they experimented with seeding with a GPS. By using the system, the colony saves time and money on fuel, seed, fertilizer and spray. This spring, the technology has made its way into our colony permanently. It is now part of our seeding routine, which has to be done to be able to make ends meet at harvest time in the fall.

A goal for the next few years is to add GPS "mapping"—a computerized layout of the fields' measurements.

I asked my brother Brian about the GPS for an article last fall. He asked me to wait and write about it this spring. "We're just learning to use it. Let us work out the bugs first," he said. Surprisingly, to the men, one of the "bugs" included the satellites guiding the system. Since the 9-11 happenings, the satellites were "out of whack," as my brother puts it.

There were no precautions taken or special remedies to outdo the drought. Seeding is done no differently than from last year and the years before; it is simply left up to hope and faith.

The men expect the job to take one week—"If we don't get rained out, which is unusual in this part of the country," says one of the guys, hiding a sarcastic smile and tired after spending a hard day at work out in the field.

Colony Pulls Together Night and Day to Get Seeding Done

Getting the seeding done at the Gildford Colony has been the excitement among the men this past week. If all goes as planned, the project takes two full weeks. But with the weather, it sometimes stretches into three.

Preparation begins a month ahead of time. The guys get all their equipment fixed up and ready for the field, and they bring the planting seed and the fertilizer home.

As seeding nears, there's always the planning and developing among the men. They'll discuss the different seed or fertilizer they'll be using or go over new plans for this season, such as new methods of seeding, etc. They're always working on improving farm technology with ideas that aren't time-consuming, and they are constantly coming up with new ideas. If the equipment they buy isn't big enough, they make it bigger themselves. Last year, they enlarged the loading augers so refilling time would be cut in half.

Every Hutterite colony farms land as one of their main income sources. The field boss is in charge of the colony's farmland. The single guys and most of the married men work under his supervision.

The boss usually gives the command to start seeding in mid-April.

If things go well, there are six guys on the day shift and three at night. The work never stops. Two men run the seeding drills, while another drives the semi with the seed and fertilizer.

The two shifts aren't quite divided by twelve hours. The guys at night usually get the longer shift, thirteen to fourteen hours. During the day, three other guys work together to do the spraying. They always have to work in twelve-hour shifts to be a day ahead of the seeders.

But if the weather doesn't cooperate, they can be held back as much as a few days. If the wind acts up too much, they can't spray, and in the morning it has to be at least fifty degrees before they can start.

I find the seeding the most fascinating.

Most of what we seed is wheat, barley, oats and sometimes winter wheat. This year we tried something new—chickpeas.

Of course, seeding also involves the women. We have to be on schedule with breakfast, lunch, supper and night buckets for both shifts.

Most of what the guys eat are sandwiches, for their convenience, so it's fun to introduce a new sandwich for variety. For supper, if possible, the cooks will send out "hot plates" for a change, instead of the same old sandwiches and chips.

Seeding is something all the guys truly enjoy. Maybe it's the thought of driving around in those huge, powerful tractors, which can seed a sixty-foot-wide swath in one shot.

Or maybe it's that secure feeling every farmer has when the job is done.

Prospective Cowboys Help with Colony Calving Duties

The sleepy cowboy reaches from beneath his warm blanket to shut off his bedside alarm. It reads 2:00 A.M.

Tossing the blanket aside, he slips into his boots and coat, grabs his flashlight from a nearby table and opens the door.

He's greeted with total darkness, and a cool breeze brushes his cheek. Now wide awake and alert, he makes his way to the dimly lighted corral several yards in the distance, to several dozen head of Black Angus ranch cows.

He enters the corral just in time to see a wet, solid-black calf take its first breath of fresh air—the newest addition to the herd at the Gildford Hutterite Colony.

At our farm the calving season lasts from the beginning of February until the end of April.

Each year two or three different guys from our colony get to help with the calving season. This way everyone can get the feel of the different jobs on the farm and someday discover where their strengths and interests lie when it comes time to take on a permanent job.

Every colony has a cow camp located a fair distance from the homes. The camp is close to the corrals where the calving takes place for the convenience of the men.

The cowboys take turns sharing the night shift so the same one isn't up each night.

If a problem should occur, such as having to assist a calf being born in the middle of the night—the other cowhand is there to help.

In the morning the men enjoy a hot breakfast at the house before they start feeding the cows.

A couple extra men from the colony will come to help, including the foreman. He'll tell the cowhands what they have to do that morning and later, when he finds some time, he'll eartag the calves born during the night and record them in the record book.

In the afternoon, the men saddle up their horses and move the mothers and their calves out to the corral to a pasture.

The corral next to the cow camp is prepared for the next set of ranch cows waiting to give birth.

The cowboys' job is routine, but occasionally they'll run into the problem of a calf having to be delivered by C-section. This is done with the assistance of one of the local vets in town.

Sometimes the mother becomes the problem by refusing to accept her own calf or adopting another cow's calf. If nature can't solve the problem, then one of the cowboys has to.

As the afternoon draws to a close and school lets out for the day, the children come to visit the newborn calves. If anyone is interested to learn how many calves have been born, they need only ask the kids. They'll not only tell you that, but also how many sets of twins we've had. I was taking a walk around the farm one afternoon with my younger sister, when she popped up with this question. "Lisa, do you know how the mommies know which one of the calves is theirs?"

Curious to hear her answer, I asked her, "How?"

"By looking at their ear tags," she answered. I smiled at her clever reply and decided to save the correct answer for when she was older and better able to understand.

Schedule Constant, Sleep Unpredictable as Calving Season Continues on Colony

It's four in the morning when I hear commotion outside my bedroom door. Curiosity wins out, and I slip out of bed to see what's happening.

I find my brother pulling on a pair of overalls, and I stop him as he gets ready to leave.

"Why aren't you sleeping?" I ask.

"We have to take a heifer in to the vet for a C-section. I just came up to the house to get dressed warmer. It's pretty cold out," he answers, and a minute later he's off.

Calving starts in early February at my colony. Unlike the other busy ranching events, the calving schedule is constant, and rest for the working cowboys is always unpredictable.

Though our guys are well-educated in the line of ranching, they aren't equipped or trained to perform C-sections on our herd of Black Angus cows, although some colonies do perform their own.

The guys' knowledge of ranching was taught to them simply by participation, and the trade is passed down from the older generation. None of them has taken veterinary courses, although occasionally they attend cow meetings in town to learn about the latest vaccinations and such.

We're about halfway through calving now, and so far we've been surprised with six sets of twins—three sets born within forty-eight hours.

The two main cowhands and foreman have a routine schedule checking on the birthing mothers. During the night one of the cowboys checks up on the cows every two hours—sometimes three if they're dealing with an old cow or heifer.

If he needs to be assisted with pulling a calf, he calls on his helper who's sharing their one-room cow camp.

The cow camp is where the guys stay overnight during the calving season. It's a cozy little building with two beds, a small kitchen and sitting room in one. It's located right next to the corral where the calving mothers are. This setup is for the convenience of the cowboys.

Under the tutelage of his dad and uncles, James Stahl tackles a calf for branding.

Because of unusually cold weather this year, every calf has had to be carted (by a calf caddy) into the barn, followed by its mom, to be dried.

Each morning the cowboys come home to eat a late breakfast (specially prepared by the cooks) before they start feeding the cows. During the day, several other guys assist them so the two steady cowhands on duty can catch up on some needed sleep.

I asked the two cowboys what their favorite part of calving was. The first answered, "Seeing a calf get up and start suckling, minutes after being born."

Thinking hard, the other replied, "Nice weather. Not having to drag the calves into the barn."

Old-fashioned Branding in New Millennium Still Treasured by Modern Colony Cowboys

I love cows. I love the calving season. But overall, my favorite is branding.

About this time each year, my colony does its annual branding. As one of our guys commented to me: "Branding at our colony is seeing the family circus come to life." It's true—the event is very comical.

Like most ranchers in our area, we brand the old-fashioned cowboy way—with horses and several sets of eager wrestlers.

Branding day is usually a spur-of-the-moment decision based on the weather. First thing in the morning, the guys separate the cows from the calves. After an early lunch in the communal kitchen they get the shots ready, start up the branding table and get the branding rods hot and ready. That done, the cowboys can start roping calves. Everybody helps on branding day.

Four guys or girls are occupied with the shots. This is the time when the calves are vaccinated, and it seems like every year there's a new shot to keep the calves from getting sick or a new improvement the guys want to try out.

But the branding is the most important part of the entire event. A few seconds of pain gets a calf its permanent "home address" on its left side. Branding is a lot of fun to watch and even more enjoyable to participate in. But it's also dangerous and physically demanding, especially the wrestling. Some of the calves weigh more than two hundred pounds, and the wrestler has to keep them pinned to the ground with his entire weight. Even the horses have work to do, dragging the roped calves in by their two hind feet.

Participants have to be alert and on the ball. You have to stay out of the way so the cows and horses don't run you over.

The cows don't much enjoy the branding.

They don't like being separated from their calves, and they don't take the event lightly. You can hear them bellowing from a distance looking for their calf. After the calves are branded and released, mother and calf are reunited.

Of course, we also have our own personal cheerleading squad among our audience.

The colony kids cheer for their dad or brother to successfully rope a calf by both its hind legs instead of just one, or to wrestle a super-heavy calf without getting bucked off.

Off the Pasture, Away from Mama, Off to Market

It's six in the morning. Most of the men are already up, preparing for the long day ahead. Several are in the horse barn, getting the horses saddled and loading them into the horse trailer. Two of the guys start the two semis so they're warmed up and ready to go with the rest of the crew.

This past week has been the busiest week for the cowboys this fall. It's shipping time for the baby calves. Most of the other men get to practice their cowboy skills, because a lot of extra help is needed to help wean the baby calves. But they're not really babies anymore. Through the summer months they've grown to be half the size of their moms, and they weigh from six hundred to seven hundred pounds.

Finally, with everyone ready, they grab a hot bacon and egg sandwich from the communal kitchen (along with a cold sandwich for lunch) made by the cooks that morning, and they're on their way.

It's about a two-hour drive to where the cattle are. Our cows are in summer pasture more than one hundred miles from my colony, since grazing pastures aren't available in our area, due to a shortage of water.

Arriving around eight or nine in the morning, the cowboys start rounding up the cows and their calves, and separate the pairs. Several dozen heads of replacement heifers are loaded into our trailers to be taken home. The rest of the calves are taken to out-of-state feedlots by the buyer.

On a good day's run, if things go smoothly and the cattle aren't too difficult to find, the cowboys can round up about two hundred head. The separation is an emotional time for both mother and calf, because neither will see the other again. Both wander around bawling for a while, looking for its mother or calf. It takes them about two days to adjust to the change.

The mothers are taken home, where they are vaccinated and pregtested. Then they're put out on wheat field pastures, fenced off by the guys earlier this summer. Since many of our fields weren't combined (it was so dry it would have been a waste of time) the cowboys are using them for pasture.

There the cows stay until a few weeks before calving season, when they're brought home to pastures on the colony. In the meantime, water is being hauled from our wells to the cattle daily, since the reservoirs are dried up.

We raise mostly Black Angus cattle. Besides farming, ranching is one of our main income sources. But in the past few years, it's been an ongoing struggle for both with the rain shortage. With no wheat crop, there's also no straw or hay to bale for the ranch cows. Lacking rainfall, the pastures available can't support the cattle they should. Poor wheat and beef prices also make the situation difficult.

It's a tough job trying to make a living off the land in the twenty-first century.

Routine Job Holds Fascination for Children

The best part of duck butchering, I remember as a kid, was inviting the schoolteacher to watch. We kids figured that was the highlight of the day! When morning recess came, we were all begging to spend our break at the slaughterhouse.

It was fascinating for us to watch back then, but when we became older and joined the other colony members in getting the job done, we realized how important it was and why we had to do it.

It wasn't just done for the fun of doing it; it was done to supply our colony with one type of meat for the upcoming winter months.

So there we were, tugging on the teacher's hand, urging her to hurry because "we might miss something."

It was a routine job, for which, after years of practice, the steps come easy.

The assembly line starts at the butcher block, where one of the men chops off the heads. This step is the bloodiest part of butchering, and we school kids always made it a point to show the teacher.

Growing up on a farm, we were used to seeing this, so we got a kick out of the expressions the teachers made. Of course, they usually grimaced and hurried away from that part of the butcher line.

The ducks are placed into a cone-shaped brace where the heads are chopped off. They are left there until they have stopped bleeding. The men put a pile of straw under the revolving cones to catch the blood.

From the butcher block, the ducks are placed in a homemade duck steamer, where they're steamed for two to three minutes.

When they're done, they're put on a long table surrounded by the young girls and boys. There, all the feathers are plucked within the next two minutes, before the duck cools off. The feathers are much harder to pull when the duck is no longer hot, so we have to be quick.

The next steps are chopping off the wings and legs, which are then dipped in wax. This is the step the kids find the most interesting. On our break, when the guy who was waxing wasn't looking, we'd make hand and finger molds to take to school.

The ducks are put into ice water to harden the wax, then the wax is peeled off, along with all the excess feathers that remained after the plucking. The wax is melted and used over and over.

Next, the ducks are gutted and put into ice water. The next morning we drain the water, pack them and put them in the freezer.

Butchering is a messy job, but with all the adult colony members present, it can be done in a matter of hours. With a teasing smirk, we've suggested each year to my dad, who's in charge of the poultry, that he purchase ducks and geese without feathers. We keep telling him that butchering would be a lot easier and faster if he would. He's yet to lose a single gray hair figuring out how.

Dry, Hot Conditions Bring Out Best in People, Worst in Snakes

Taking an evening ride with my brother to where one of the guys waits to switch shifts swathing, I closed my eyes at the sight of our wheat crops burning up under the heat. Because of lack of moisture, the wheat heads couldn't fill out properly and wouldn't yield as much.

Along the way, we spotted a coiled rattlesnake in the middle of the road. Slowing down, my brother angled the front left tire for its center— squashing it instantly. "That's the fourth one I've driven over this year," he commented as he got out of the car to check if he had killed it.

It's been our third dry year. The guys decided to swath most of the wheat fields and bale it up for the ranch cows to eat this coming winter. This way the sun and lack of rain won't do anymore damage.

Since farming is one of our main income sources, it lays a heavy burden on our present outlook. With the low wheat prices, more and more farmers are selling out. Farming is slowly becoming an extinct profession. It's a saddening thought, since it's one of our most important livelihoods.

As for the bigger farmers, they're starting to wonder if it's worth spending all this money on seeds, fertilizer and maintenance of their equipment if they can't make ends meet in the fall.

Unlike last summer, we were blessed with a garden this season. Though we can't irrigate, it's come a surprisingly long way with the low rainfall this spring. Our reservoirs have been dry for two years now, so only through the grace and love of God has our garden survived. So far our ladies have been kept busy picking peas, beets, loose-leaf lettuce, spinach, etc.

Whatever will not yield won't be a complete loss to us. Our many neighboring colonies will help us out—just as they did last year and just as my own colony has helped out in past years. Last summer we were helped out with produce by seventeen colonies—both from Montana and Canada.

I guess what worries me most is the welfare of the children. Because of lack of rain, rattlesnakes have been coming right to our front doors in search of water. I'm constantly warning my little sisters and their friends to be careful of where they play during the day and to stay out of high grass and away from rocks.

With August just around the corner, I'm concerned about the snakes' shedding period. They are considered to be "blind" because their skin covers their eyes. They can't see, and they strike at anything.

I got my biggest scare when my cousin found a fully-grown rattler in my front yard about two weeks back. Without nature's warning, my cousin might have stepped right on it, because it camouflages so easily.

Even though we are encountering some difficult times, we all must stick together waiting for a positive outcome. But most importantly, we must not lose faith in the Lord and believe in His assuring guidance, even if He says "no."

Good Riddance to this Dry, Dreary Summer

On September 2, I saw the first Canada goose fly south to its winter resort—somewhere in Florida or Arizona, perhaps. I smiled at the thought of summer ending and the cool months of fall ahead of us.

I never wanted a summer to end as much as this one. I just couldn't bear the sight of the dry, dreary look out here in the country anymore. I thought perhaps the fall colors would brighten people's spirits.

Our garden was a growing miracle this year. Though much of the early summer produce yielded poorly or not at all, our fall vegetables prospered unbelievably.

I never knew zucchini, squash, melons or pumpkins could grow without water, but it happened this year. Our watermelons and cantaloupes didn't grow to be very big, but they were as sweet as sugar.

One afternoon we went to the garden for some vegetables and discovered a banana squash that had grown to the length of three feet! We showed it to everyone at home, and each time we got the same question: Which colony can grow squash to be that big? They all gave us a "I know you're kidding me" chuckle when we answered, "Ours."

Of course, since not very many of the other vegetables survived the dry summer, many of the colonies had to help us out again this year. More than a dozen from Montana and Canada donated produce. We were able to can all the vegetables we'll be needing for the next year.

With canning behind us, our summer is coming to a close. We're finishing up all the autumn activities to prepare for the upcoming winter.

In the months of September and October, all the fall butchering takes place so we can fill the freezer for winter. We already butchered the ducks, chickens, beef and pigs. In October we'll butcher the geese, and we'll make sausage in November.

Then the meat processing will be finished.

In the next two weeks, our ladies will tackle the job of fall cleaning all the colony buildings. Later, each will also fall-clean her own home.

After that, we'll settle back and enjoy the winter months, with hopes of loads and loads of snow. The ladies will take this time to go home to their maiden colonies to visit with family and friends. They'll also have lots of time to get their sewing done, since there is hardly any time to do that during the spring and summer.

The men also will take on indoor projects in the mechanic and carpentry shop. Already this fall, they've started working on new playground equipment. They'll fix up their farming equipment so that it's as good as new.

The cowboys will bring the ranch cows home to the colony to get ready for the calving season, which won't be until mid-winter.

Of course, the children will be nice and snug in school—a safe place for them to be.

Now, it's time to put our minds to ease and thank the Lord for keeping us safe another year. And with the best thoughts of the future and a positive outlook, we'll hope and pray for a wonderful, fruitful next year.

But first, we'll live the present.

Joy of Bringing in Harvest
Dries Up in Summer Heat

Harvest is an exciting event that everyone looks forward to at the end of summer. Unfortunately, this year the excitement and joy of bringing in the yearly crop just wasn't there.

Normally, harvest takes from three weeks to more than a month. This year, we were done in less than a week. The guys cut most of what they thought looked good enough to run the combines through and left the rest standing. Some fields they fenced off to put the ranch cows on later this fall.

Before they started, the guys knew roughly what to expect from the fields—five to ten bushels an acre. In most cases, they were right on.

Joining my brother for a truck ride in the evening, I took notice of his gloomy state of mind right away. It seemed like he couldn't get into the mood of things. I missed the laughter, the sparkle in his eyes and that usual hasty voice of, "Come on and get into the truck if you want a ride. The guys are already waiting for me in the field."

I tried to imagine this year's crop like the ones we had about half a decade ago. That was back when the winter wheat was almost high enough to hide in, standing up; back when the wheat would lean over from the weight of the fully filled heads.

Back then, harvest time wasn't such a rat race. Everyone had the same push to get the harvest in as fast as possible. But things were done so differently compared to how they're done today.

Before individual lunch and supper buckets to "eat on the go" became popular, harvest meals were enjoyed with the company of all the crew members.

The ladies took pride in preparing a wheat field picnic twice a day.

When suppertime was announced over the CBs, the guys driving the combines would park their equipment in a circle. The cooks spread out a large white picnic blanket and laid out the food with the help of one or two of us school kids who were always begging to be taken along to "help the cooks take supper out to the combine guys."

The men enjoyed a hot supper with their fellow workers with no worries of "Hustle up, boys. We have to keep those engines running and moving."

It was always fun to cook during harvest time, even though there was more work involved. The cooks would also make a special snack to take out to the guys, along with a pop, for an afternoon and midnight snack.

I recall when the girls had the choice of sharing rides with three different truck drivers, unlike this year when only one of the semi trucks was needed.

I'm not sure how long this dry period will last or what the cause of it all is. But perhaps if we'd stop for a moment to think things through, maybe God is just putting us to a test to see if our faith will outlast the drought. We pray that next year things will be different.

I miss the harvests of yesteryear.

Every Drop of Rain Welcome Despite Damage

Do you believe in miracles? I do. The area around my colony has been in a four-year drought. For the past few years, our crop has failed. So has our garden.

The miracle of rain was almost unheard-of in northcentral Montana, until Saturday, June 8.

The rain came soft and gentle. My mom said this is the first time in her life she's seen it rain nonstop for four days. That's what I call a miracle.

The last two summers, our guys worked at enlarging all our dried-out reservoirs. I heard one of the men comment once, "Maybe God has a reason to dry out the reservoirs, so we can enlarge them for something bigger that's yet to come."

The five inches of rain we received were welcomed and every drop was appreciated. The rain filled up most of the reservoirs, including the one at our garden. It's such a blessing to know we'll be able to irrigate and have our own garden this year.

But for some of our neighbors in Canada, the storm turned threatening overnight.

At the Spring Creek Colony in Alberta, just eighty miles north of the Wild Horse border crossing, it started raining Saturday afternoon. It didn't let up until Tuesday night, after a total of ten inches fell. The creek behind the colony overflowed.

This time, the colony was prepared.

Seven years ago, in the spring of 1995, the colony had a similar flood. Unprepared at the time, they had to take their ducks and geese to a neighboring colony fifteen miles away and pump water out of their houses and the communal kitchen's basement.

In 1995, the colony made a four-foot dike around the creek to prevent flooding on the colony, said resident Rhoda Hofer, age eighteen. This time, the colony didn't have to transport any of its livestock. In fact, when the town of Walsh flooded on Monday, colony members helped move animals from town to the colony, to safe ground.

Farther west, the Pincher Creek Colony received six inches of rain and six inches of good, wet snow—a total of ten inches of moisture, said Mike Gross, age sixty-two, the colony's financial boss. The sudden heavy snow caused tree branches to bend and break off.

"There was a lot of tree damage," Gross said.

But this was not the worst damage. Farther to the east, the Standoff Colony sits between two rivers—the Belly and the Waterton. The rain seems to have hit them the hardest.

Though the colony only received seven inches of rain, it made the rivers in the area overflow, said resident Lisa Wipf, age eighteen. They had to move their cows and sheep to higher pasture, since their sheep and cow camp is in a valley right next to the Waterton River.

The rain washed out their garden. It also damaged bits and pieces of their wheat crop. "If it's not too late, the colony will reseed the garden and maybe even the wheat fields," Wipf said.

The colony is keeping a watchful eye on the two rivers. In 1995, they were unprepared when the gates to the Waterton River, at Old Man River Dam, had to be opened because of the sudden rains. They had no warning, and the damage was much worse.

If the three feet of snow that fell earlier this week in the mountains melts suddenly, the gates will have to be opened, and chances of the colony flooding will be high.

For the last two years, Standoff Colony has had a drought. Most of their dams were dried up. But with the rain, they are filled up and ready to overflow.

Some colonies, like the Elkwater Colony thirty miles southeast of Medicine Hat, Alberta, received twelve inches of rain. There was some damage but nothing more than a little water in the colony homes' basements. "Even though it came fast, it did more good than damage," the Rev. Paul Hofer said.

This colony, along with sixty other farmers, has a line from Elkwater Lake to take water for their livestock. The Alberta government was on the verge of cutting the farmers off because the lake was so low.

"We've had two dry years, but with the twelve inches of rain we received, the lake is filled up and we're allowed to use the water from the lake," Hofer said. "We're thankful and grateful for the rain."

Colonies such as Lakeside, near Cranford, Alberta, received more than nine inches of rain. It was welcomed with a cheerful smile. They were grateful for the moisture, welcoming every drop.

"The rain has been a blessing," Andy Wipf said.

So overall, June is off to an excellent start.

We can't thank God enough for the beautiful rain he sends us. He hasn't forgotten about us after all. I hope and pray that the rest of the summer will be just as pleasant and inviting.

Rain Creates Much to be Appreciated in Nature

I just can't seem to get enough of nature this summer. It seems that each day I discover something new that amazes me. The biggest miracle of all is the water that ran into our empty reservoirs in June when the rains finally came.

When we saw the drought was taking a turn for the best, we decided it wasn't a good idea to ignore nature's call this time.

My grandpa, who is the colony's gardener, had been discussing all year long the possibility of installing a "drip system" for our garden.

When planting time came in May, things weren't looking up.

Hauling water from our well was a possibility but not a perfect solution.

June had a different answer though. When my grandpa saw all the water that had accumulated in our garden reservoir after the June rains, he knew he could go ahead and install the drip system.

He did and has had some great success with it all summer. In fact, I haven't seen our garden so beautiful, healthy and green for the longest time.

We have a feeling of appreciation now when we weed, hoe and pick vegetables in our garden. It's a change not to have to worry about where we'll get our winter supply of frozen and canned vegetables.

The ladies are all enjoying the vegetable canning this summer. The men did some remodeling in our slaughterhouse (where we also do the canning) for the convenience of the ladies, so that adds to the joy of canning, as well.

On August 1, we started up our farmers' market in Big Sandy, which we've been doing for two years now. On Thursday mornings we get up to bake fresh buns, bread, peas and other pastries which we pack for that evening market. We also pack fresh vegetables like potatoes, head lettuce, zucchini, beets and cucumbers to take along.

Market starts at five and is to last until 6:30. But within a half-hour, the crowd that has gathered and is waiting for us has cleaned out all the freshly baked pastries, potatoes and most of the other vegetables.

Back home on the colony, the men-talk turns serious about the crop, which has rapidly turned to harvest gold. Waiting to be put to use, the combines that were fixed up a month ago are parked in front of the garage.

Until the time comes, the men are busy trying to finish up baling the CRP they swatted down after it was released to farmers and ranchers several weeks ago. Each day the bale stacks behind the colony grow and grow.

The guys feel pretty blessed to have been able to cut the colony's winter supply of hay within a twenty-mile radius of the colony instead of two hundred miles away as they had to last year.

We've all been blessed this year. The rain has not only done some wonderful things for the land but also for the people's spirits.

Cooks Offer Proper Fuel to Help Colony Men Stay on Top of Harvest

I'm cooking this week. Harvest time is going strong and steady, so already Monday morning, I knew to expect a hectic week.

July, August and September are the busiest time of year on the colony. And it's just as busy for the women as it is for the men.

During harvest time, mornings for the cooks start around five. We are up preparing breakfast, as well as getting a headstart on the noon meal.

Because of harvest, meal preparation is a bit different than usual. Around 9:30, we get a count of the number of lunch buckets to make for the harvest crew. They are finished and ready to be distributed to each of the men by eleven o'clock.

Not only is the meal preparation different, but the menu also changes a lot during harvest time. Being well aware of the men's food choices, the ladies try to come up with different sandwich recipes each year to liven up the variety. Some of the most popular are roast beef, clubhouse, submarine and ham and cheese.

Making "buckets" tends to be an easy task. But occasionally, it does become a memory game when the guys call in their "special requests." When the guys get a chance to know ahead of time what's on the menu for that day, they'll let the cooks know their order has been slightly changed, with the requests of extra mayonnaise, no mustard, carrot and cucumber sticks, if possible, and maybe an extra bag of chips.

Once in awhile, when we're caught up with our work and we feel like being extra nice, the cooks will fix milkshakes for the guys or make them a treat of Rice Krispies squares and caramel wheat puffs for an evening snack.

During fuel-up time, the guys make it a habit to take their empty pop cans and disposable buckets to the fuel pickup, where an empty built-in garbage can is always waiting. They try their best to keep the wheat fields junk-free.

When an occasional rain interrupts the guys' combining schedule,

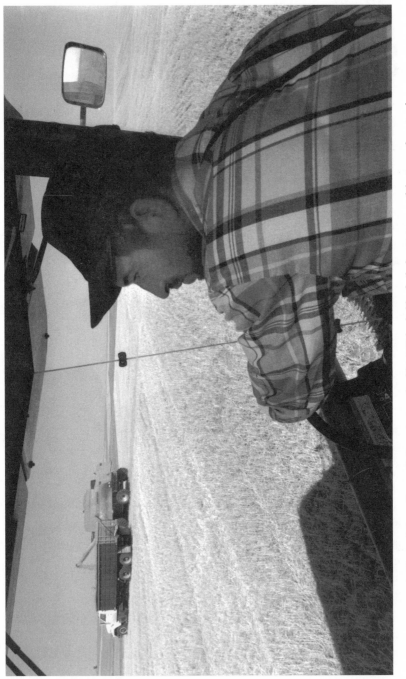

At Turner Colony, Danny Hofer waits to unload his 350-bushel load of wheat into one of the two colony trucks.

they have to quit. But that doesn't necessarily give the cooks a break. The guys just switch from combining to hauling bales, and we still have our normal number of buckets to prepare.

So far, it's been a great harvest season, despite the occasional change of the weather pattern. On a good night, the men sometimes work until two in the morning. But the evenings are cool this fall, which makes it difficult for them to combine later than eleven, or sometimes even earlier, because the wheat gets "tough." In the mornings, they also can't get started until at least nine o'clock because of the night's dew and too much moisture in the wheat heads.

Of course, now that school has started for the colony kids, the guys have less on their minds. Harvest being as exciting as it is, the kids find it a treat to join the men for a truck and combine ride. It was something they had missed out on the last few years because drought damaged our harvest, so they take every opportunity to join the fun.

Honestly, I think everyone on the colony looks forward to the harvest. It's such an exciting time. And somewhere along the way, everyone, young and old, finds they have a part in it.

Which reminds me, I'd better sign off now and head for the kitchen. There are about ten supper buckets to be made for a hungry harvest crew.

With her sister Rhoda at her side, Lisa Marie Stahl works on her word processor in her downstairs room.

The Writing Life

A Look Back: Writing a Column is a Pleasure on Many Different Levels

January 2 marked the first anniversary of my column in the *Great Falls Tribune*. Of course, I wasn't new to the media, since many already knew me from the *Havre Daily News*.

In my honest opinion, it was a great year. I started out writing once a month and then switched to once every two weeks.

I'm really enjoying the responses I'm getting from my column because it lets me know that my articles are being read. And the responses I'm getting are overwhelmingly positive.

So far, I've received more than one hundred letters from readers.

I'm always intrigued by what people write, and occasionally, by what they send me. For example, last Christmas, when the *Tribune* interviewed me, I called my editor, asking her to send me copies. She helped me out but was sorry to say there were only six copies left.

To my amazement, a week later, I had received close to a dozen copies of the paper from readers who felt the article was a keepsake, enough to part with their own copy. (How thoughtful of people, whom I've never even met, to do that.)

Once an elderly lady from Great Falls wrote me about a wonderful Hutterite friend she had met but later lost contact with. Through her descriptions, I was able to reunite the two friends. According to a later letter, they are now corresponding and have distant plans to meet again.

It's always an inspiration when someone writes from out of state. As a matter of fact, I'm guessing that one-third of the letters I've received are from outside Montana. I'm amazed that my column finds its way to Oregon, Washington, North Dakota, South Dakota, Colorado, California and also Canada.

But what I'm always touched by is when people write to thank me for taking on the responsibility of informing the public about my culture. And it thoroughly is a responsibility. I feel it is my duty to answer people's questions when they write me, to help them out with their essay projects and give them an understanding of aspects of Hutterite life that have kept them puzzled.

Sometimes my readers inspire me. I came home from a busy day in the communal kitchen and discovered a recent column of mine lying on our kitchen table—neatly cut and laminated. After inquiring about where it came from, I learned that our schoolteacher had laminated it for me, because, I assumed, of her thoughts on the importance of the topic.

At that moment, I made my first New Year's resolution—I was going to search for, copy, cut, paste (whatever it took) every article I have written, for the *Tribune* and the *Daily News*, and make a book for my personal record and memorabilia. This was some of the advice I am always getting from my readers. And finally someone decided to give me a push-start.

Thanks, Mrs. Kuhn, for the reminder.

Hutterite Columnist Celebrates Two Years

I can't believe it! On January 2, it was two years since I started my column with the *Tribune*. What an incredible year it has been. I was able to cover so many topics, and surprisingly I haven't run out of ideas yet.

As a matter of fact, I still have a few stashed away in the back of my mind. Not to mention a few my editor has been bugging me to write about—at the top of her list is the clothing differences between the three groups of Hutterites, specifically the two groups who reside in Montana.

I can't thank my readers enough for taking the time to write me notes of encouragement, and for the many Christmas cards I received last month. My readers and my family are my greatest inspiration.

I've made many lasting relationships through my column. I'm even corresponding with a teacher from Alberta who works at two Hutterite colonies. One student writes me regularly of his doings, sharing with me bits and pieces of his life through his letters.

After almost four years of writing, my family still inspires me. As you might have noticed, my three sisters never seem to tire of having their names mentioned in my column. My editor also has shown a lot of support and is always willing to lend a listening ear.

Although I can't answer all the questions and requests I get from readers, I do try. My column is only a pastime, so my colony duties and responsibilities must come first.

But don't let this stop you from asking, because you'll never know the answer unless you do.

Column Was Enriched with Support from Family, Friends and Readers

I've got a sad feeling inside me as I write my final column. I sort of feel like I'm letting my readers down by cutting off a resource that they've been relying on for the past three years.

January 2 marked my third anniversary of writing for the *Great Falls Tribune*.

Since the first Sunday my column was published, I haven't had a single regret. I feel what I did was for the benefit of the colony and the community beyond.

I can't thank God enough for choosing me to take on the challenge of writing a "Hutterite column." He was there to help me along every step of the way, many times bringing words and ideas to a blank computer screen. So often I remember He brought ideas to my mind and helped me develop them into a presentable column for my readers to read and learn from.

I thoroughly believe such a challenge comes along only once in a person's life, and it's up to the individual to use it to the best of his or her ability. Certain gifts would be a waste to let go, especially if they come from a higher power.

Many of you might have wondered how I always found topics to write about.

Sometimes I had a list of six or seven ideas stashed away in the back of my mind; other times, though, when my parents weren't able to help me out, I'd call the *Tribune* and have a brainstorming session with my editor.

Once on her day off I was pressed for an idea (I was on deadline and worried), so I called the *Tribune* in hopes of an answer. By now the people in the newsroom had gotten to know me. The receptionist who answered the phone asked around the newsroom and supplied me with not one, but several questions people wanted answered about Hutterite culture.

My work often caused me to question and research traditions in our daily Hutterite lives that I took for granted: things like why we wear a scarf to cover our heads, why our church has no decorations or musical instruments, and even why the language we speak in our homes cannot be found in written text.

Though many of you might not know, I've been writing publicly for five years. I started my column with the *Havre Daily News* at the age of fifteen. This last column is the seventy-second I've written for the *Great Falls Tribune*, with 151 altogether.

Since I announced I would quit writing four weeks ago, I've gotten more than one hundred farewell letters. Altogether, I've gotten more than six hundred letters, many of them from out of state. Several were from out of the country.

I'm always touched by what people write. The majority of letters were from older people, and many shared the same themes.

As one reader put it, "I read your column this morning as I do every Sunday morning. I got tears in my eyes as I read it. I am so happy with the choices you have made, but I will miss you and your column very much. It's like losing a friend and never knowing about the rest of her life."

My only wish, as I close this chapter in my life, would be to find someone willing to start another "Hutterite column," not from my perspective, but theirs. I'm sure there are many more topics of interest that need to be touched on and explained.

The Hutterite way of life is truly an amazing culture, as many readers have told me. As a Great Falls resident wrote, "Sometimes after reading your stories, I find myself somewhat envious of your lifestyle, and I congratulate you and your family for continuing that way of life in this so-called 'modern' society."

So I'd like to express my sincerest thanks for the many, many words of encouragement, for cheering me up and putting a smile on my face. I'd also like to thank my parents and my family for supporting me and being at my side.

Once and for all, I must wish you all "goodbye." Thank you for letting me be a part of your life, even if for only a little while.

The happy wedding couple, Lisa Marie Stahl and Ben Tschetter,
on their wedding day, June 15, 2003.

My Wedding

"I saw him from a distance . . . our eyes met. Slowly, gently a hidden smile slipped into view. The moment turned to a dream. A dream turned into a memory. Then suddenly, I heard a bell ring in Heaven, and I knew my heart was his."

This was the verse that introduced my wedding invitation. I had spent many hours working on the invitation—designing it, arranging the flowers (which were also part of my bouquet), and writing the words myself.

Two years after Ben Tschetter proposed to me, I was finally living the dream I had dreamed about for so long—my very own wedding was about to take place. I was just three weeks shy of my twenty-first birthday.

Throughout the winter months, I had slaved away sewing my wedding dresses and three sets of clothes for the nine members of my family, including the groom. It is customary for a bride to sew both her clothes and the groom's for their wedding.

The reality of my wedding hit me about two weeks before the scheduled date, when several of my best friends, cousins, and aunts came to help me with my packing, making squares, a type of dessert bar, for my tea party, and preparing our house for many guests.

I knew the routine by heart. I had been to enough Hutterite weddings to know. Yet no wedding was the same. Each had its own special surprises waiting.

My three younger sisters seemed to struggle with the fact that they'd be losing a family member. Though they seemed to accept it and showed openly that they already missed me—though I wasn't yet gone—there were times when one of them would put on "the brakes" and for an hour refuse to help me with my packing and just sneak away quietly to be alone.

Things won't be the same. It isn't like when a brother is married. He usually just moves across the street, and when he becomes a certain age, you're ready to kick him out of the nest anyway. When a sister is married, she moves to another colony, in my case, to another country.

My brothers—well, they teased me about being so ignorant as to give up my single life and of course complained about all the boxes of my "treasures" they had to help me pack, load and unload.

My parents quietly accepted my decision, and at certain moments, when they thought I wasn't looking, I saw them wipe away a tear or two.

Tuesday

For my colony, the excitement began on Tuesday afternoon. I had posted an invitation at the communal kitchen inviting the ladies to my tea party that afternoon in the kitchen dining room. It was my final reunion with the ladies, and in a personal way it was like giving my last farewell to them before the REAL excitement would start the next evening.

The girls who I had asked to come help with my preparations the week before had set up the dining room just for the occasion. A large table was loaded with squares, treats, and beverages. My three special hostesses, my sister Rhoda and Rhoda's friends Brittany and Kathleen, delivered treats and drinks to the ladies and took care of their dirty plates.

Then, as was planned, my best friends started up several games prepared for the occasion. I made up a series of questions for one game called "How Well Do You Know Lisa?" The ladies also wrote on pieces of paper "Advice for the Bride." Several door prizes were awarded, and just before the party came to an end, the young girls delivered a small gift to each colony lady—gifts my sister-in-law Rosa and I had made several months in advance.

That night was a restless evening for me because my mind often lingered on the events of the following day. With the few helpers and wedding guests already there, things were moving quickly.

Wednesday

Wednesday found me up early, as sleep was the furthest thing from my mind. I had talked with Ben the night before, and he'd secretly told me when to expect him and the other guys who would be accompanying him on his trip to my colony.

Shortly after breakfast, activities started buzzing at the kitchen, and food was already in preparation for the big supper we'd be having that evening. The guys set up tables, benches, and chairs in the dining room for enough seating for all the guests who'd be coming for the shivaree the next evening. There was no official shivaree on Wednesday evening, just a big supper.

At the front center of the dining room there were two cushioned chairs, reserved for the bride and groom. Tonight Ben and I would be the honored guests, and our wedding party would sit to the left and right, with the guests at the remaining tables.

The clock moved slowly that morning. Finally, the dinner bell rang, and we sat down for a light lunch of sandwiches. I had no appetite. I kept looking out the window, hoping to see a gray Ford crewcab with a trailer hooked to the back. At least that was the vehicle description Ben had given me the night before. "Expect me some time between one and two tomorrow afternoon," he had said. I could hear the excitement in his voice.

My sister Rhoda seemed to be more excited than I because it

seemed to burst out of her. Her cheeks were a soft pink, and hard as she tried at times, she couldn't hide her large smile. Whenever she saw me, she'd pull me into a hug and whisper, "When is he gonna come?"

She must have been on the watch for me, because shortly before one o'clock, she burst into the house, unable to control her excitement. "He's here. I saw him drive in!"

My heart raced wild as I tried to push my way through my five bridesmaids toward the window so I could catch a peek of him. He was driving, and although he didn't see me, I caught his smiling face as soon as he exited the pickup.

I met him on the porch, and for half a minute, the world stopped as we looked into each other's eyes. "For you," he whispered as he handed me a dozen red roses. As I reached for them, I was pulled into a warm hug. The crowd around us cheered. Then, taking his hand, I invited him into the house.

* * * * * * * * * *

While Ben and I got dressed for that evening's shivaree (I wore a teal satin dress), Ben's dad did his fatherly duty and delivered a handwritten letter to my grandpa, the colony's minister. This letter was written by the minister at the Estuary Colony explaining that Ben had come and asked for spiritual guidance regarding the steps that one must follow to get married.

A meeting was called at four o'clock that afternoon, which only the brothers of the church were allowed to attend. Ben was also asked to attend. Each brother had the chance to say whether or not he was in favor of allowing the wedding to proceed.

Following this meeting was a family gathering at my home, and the next step of the wedding—aufreden—took place. This German term refers to asking the family for the bride's hand in marriage.

This meeting is a very emotional time for the bride's family. My dad didn't care to hide his tears, although my brothers tried. Each family member got the chance to say if they were willing to give me to Ben. They gave advice on how to resolve disagreements, how to take care of each other, but most importantly, how to invite God into the center of our marriage.

Following this meeting, which lasted an hour, I quickly changed into my wedding dress and joined Ben and my wedding party for ge-bete, the evening prayer meeting. We'd be rehearsing our wedding vows, and it's customary that a bride wear her wedding dress for this special occasion. Rehearsing our wedding vows also meant we were allowed to publicly hold hands.

Supper followed the evening prayer meeting. We were served stuffed chicken and several side dishes. The guys did the serving, both food and beverages, as is the Hutterite custom.

The evening slowly came to an end with a snack served at the kitchen around nine o'clock. Several choirs sang, and the wedding guests conversed amongst themselves.

Thursday

By the time I awoke Thursday morning, our house was full of activity and people. Several of my helpers were busy registering gifts, while others did light housecleaning.

Around nine that morning, we gathered up a dozen guys or so and started packing my belongings into the horse trailer that Ben had brought along. Though I only supervised, I was there the whole time making sure that all I had packed was put into the trailer. Ben wasn't allowed to help, as he was the groom. I watched him as he shook his head, wondering how one person could accumulate so much stuff in just twenty years. I think he also secretly said a prayer, hoping that everything would fit into the trailer.

Lunch was announced at 11:30. The cooks served the food buffet style. Later that afternoon, the wedding guests started to arrive, and around 3:30, Ben and I started getting ready for the big evening. I wore a wine-colored satin dress, and most of the wedding guests wore that color as well, except they wore crepe instead of satin. Ben wore a white cotton shirt and black dress pants.

Lisa's family helps move her belongings into her new home at Estuary Colony.

The evening prayer meeting was at 5:30, and supper followed shortly thereafter. It was my favorite—Chinese food.

After supper Ben and I went home to get ready for the next custom in our schedule, giving a toast to all the wedding guests. This step was routine. The couple starts at the ministers' houses. I carried a silver plate with six silver mugs (the size of a shot glass) neatly arranged, with a red rose laying on the center of the plate. Ben carried a bottle of mixed drinks. At each house Ben filled the shot glasses, and after each person had taken one, they'd give us a wedding blessing. There was a mixture of well wishes and advice, some of it was humorous to lighten the mood.

This event took over an hour, and after we finished at the last house we hurried home to get ready for that evening's snack. It was scheduled to start at nine o'clock.

Before the snack was served, song books were passed around and several German songs were sung. Occasionally an English song was mixed in. The singing proceeded while the snacks were served. Then, suddenly, out of the crowd burst several wedding guests dressed in strange clothes to perform a skit called "Found a Peanut." A few songs later, a young man stood up and started opening a "Surprise Package." This package was wrapped in layers of newspaper. On each layer there was a joke specifically addressed to a colony member.

The singing proceeded late into the night. It was around one o'clock the next morning when Ben and I retired for the night, as cheers from the wedding guests chanted around us.

Friday

I was awakened at six o'clock Friday morning by my mother who was in the midst of doing light housekeeping and making sure my sisters' suitcases were packed for the weekend ahead.

Ben, my wedding party, and I joined the rest of the colony members at the communal kitchen for breakfast. After we had finished eating, I did what I had dreaded the most of my entire wedding. I was to go to each house (with Ben at my side) and bid everyone farewell. This was the most emotional part of my wedding for me because I had to tear my heart away from the only place I had ever known as home. I was crying the whole time, but Ben kept a firm hold of my hand and encouraged me to go on.

We were scheduled to leave at eight o'clock that morning, but my personal goodbyes took longer than I had expected. My editor from the *Great Falls Tribune*, Karen Ogden, joined us for the occasion because it was a personal request from me. She traveled along with the wedding party, entrusted with my pet beta fish, Harry.

We arrived at the Port of Wild Horse around 9:30. Ben and I were leading the caravan because I was traveling with the horse trailer that carried all my earthly possessions. I had all the right customs papers, which I had filled out months ahead. The officer on duty jotted down the information she needed and half an hour later we were on our way—off to Medicine Hat, where we'd be meeting more wedding guests to join us for the rest of the journey to Leader, Saskatchewan.

My uncle, Reverend Paul Hofer of the Elkwater Colony, had arranged lunch for us, ordering Kentucky Fried Chicken and picking out a park where we could eat. By this time there were more than sixty people with the wedding party.

We arrived in Leader some time after three that afternoon and went straight to the town hall to pick up our marriage license. By now I was getting very nervous because the Estuary Colony is only fifteen miles from Leader. When Ben and I exited the town hall, there was a surprise waiting for us. While we were inside, my five brides-maids and other wedding guests had decorated our van with stream-ers, balloons, ribbons, and pompoms in my wedding colors—purple and yellow.

The caravan stuck close together as we neared the colony. There was yet another surprise waiting; just outside the colony's yard was a flatbed trailer with straw bales, balloons, and cheering children on top, pulled by an ATV. Two young girls who I recognized as Ben's un-married sisters were holding a sign that read, "Welcome home, Ben and Lisa."

The caravan stopped at Ben's parents' home. We were first greeted with hugs and kisses by his mother, sisters, and brothers, and then by all the ladies at the Estuary Colony, each of them whispering to me, "Welcome to your new home." Also upon our arrival, I immediately became "Aunt Lisa" to Ben's eighteen nieces and nephews.

I was touched and overflowing with happiness, and I choked back tears of joy. From that moment on I knew that this was the plan God had for my life. He had planted me here at Estuary, and I was home now.

After a short snack at Ben's parents' house, Ben took me across the yard to our new home. I was excited as I looked around, trying to take in everything with one glance. I tried to contain my excitement as I went from room to room, looking and searching.

That evening the Estuary ladies made a supper of liquid-smoked chicken and several side dishes. Once again the ladies welcomed me, this time with a song called "Welcome, Welcome, From All of Us." There was no official shivaree that evening, but all the wedding guests got a chance to get acquainted with the folks at Estuary Colony.

Saturday

Saturday night was the scheduled time for the big shivaree at Estuary. In the afternoon the rest of the wedding guests arrived.

Sometime that afternoon our wedding cake was set up in our new home, made by one of the ladies at Estuary. It was a bridesmaid cake, with four bridesmaid couples surrounding the bride and groom. As I requested, the cake was decorated in purple and yellow.

The evening prayer meeting was at six o'clock that evening, and I sat in the fourth aisle with the rest of the bench taken up by my bridesmaids and Ben's sisters. Ben sat across the aisle from me with my brothers, his brothers and several friends who were among the groomsmen.

Supper followed the evening prayer meeting. Again one of my favorite dishes was served, teriyaki beef and honey-garlic-glazed hotwings.

After supper Ben and I got ready for the toasting ceremony at his

Lisa's family gathers for the wedding ceremony and celebration.

colony. We walked from house to house with our bridesmaids and bestmen trailing behind us.

We were tired by the time we got to the last house, as there were twenty homes, but the evening was far from ending for us. Soon we were ushered off to the kitchen again for the evening snack party. Lots of German wedding songs were sung, with a few English songs mixed in here and there. Soloists courageous enough to go up to the mike shared their beautiful voices with the large crowd.

The singing proceeded late into the night. After one the next morning, my mom threw a stern look my way indicating that it was time to retire for the night. In just a few short hours we'd be at the church where the actual ceremony would take place.

Sunday

I awoke Sunday morning to sunshine spilling through the window into the room that I shared with my five best friends. It was their duty to stay with me as guides and maids throughout the wedding. They were sleeping soundly when I woke them, urging them to get dressed and ready for church, which was to start in an hour and a half.

My cheeks were warm from excitement, and I couldn't hide my smile as I dressed in my sapphire-blue wedding dress. It glittered and shone with every move I made; no one would mistake me for a wedding guest.

My wedding party, Ben and I walked to the minister's house shortly before the service started, where we were given instructions on what to do at church when we were exchanging our vows.

At exactly nine o'clock, the service began. It was a beautiful sermon, telling the wedding story from Ephesians Chapter 5, read in German.

At around 10:30, the moment finally arrived. Ben and I were called by our German names to the front of the church. We were asked a series of questions. The last question we answered together. Then the minister asked for both of us to take the other's right hand, which symbolized we were now one. Laying his hand on ours he gave us the wedding blessing.

As we emerged from the church, people were waiting for us back at Ben's parents' home. During the service several ladies had set up a table outside with plastic shot glasses making a design of a heart outlined with two letters, B and L.

I was greeted by my new family, starting with my new mom and dad. My parents were crying as they embraced Ben and me in a tight hug. My brothers whispered words of love in my ear as they hugged me and quietly wiped away tears.

Soon after, the lunch bell rang, and Ben and I were once again sitting at the front of the kitchen. But lunch was served differently this time. Ben and I shared the same bowl and plate, and our wine glasses were tied together. We were allowed a spoon and fork, but no knife, because a knife symbolizes division.

While we were eating lunch, someone delivered a fax to us covered with signatures and well wishes from the ladies and children of Gildford.

After lunch, everyone gathered at our new home to take wedding pictures, first with the wedding cake and then outside.

At three o'clock that afternoon, we were served a snack, and all of the guests received a package of candy. Ben's and my package arrived in a basket neatly decorated.

That afternoon my family started setting up housekeeping and putting my wedding gifts to use around the house. The men did carpentry work, installing ceiling fans and putting together the furniture I had brought from home.

Later, we had a late supper of pizza. Most of the guests left after supper, with just my family staying behind to help me settle in.

At last the moment had come. Ben and I were to be together forever. We had been able to share this moment with our families and best friends, but mostly importantly, with God.